NERUDA, Pablo. A New Decade (Poems: 1958–67), ed. with an intro. by Ben Belitt, trans. by Ben Belitt and Alastair Reid. text in English and Spanish. Grove, 1969. 274p bibl 68-58155. 8.50

The Chilean Neruda is Latin America's leading living poet, whom Latin Americans and most Hispanists consider worthy of the Nobel Prize. He has been translated effectively for a decade or two and his poems have appeared in magazines and anthologies. Now his more recent poems (1958–67) are available in an attractive edition, with Spanish and English texts. Only poets can translate poetry so Neruda chose two for the task, Belitt and Reid. Both are fully conversant with Spanish and rarely depart from an accurate translation unless the poetic form demands it. Perhaps slightly more felicitous is Reid, the Scots writer, better known for his lucid prose than for his poetry. Preceding the poems Belitt presents the most erudite study of Neruda's poetry that has yet appeared in English. But even the novice can savor the simple, elemental concepts found in Neruda. All college libraries and most high school and public libraries should acquire the book as more and more acquaintance with Latin American culture is desired.

PABLO NERUDA

A NEW DECADE
(Poems: 1958–1967)

Edited with an Introduction by
Ben Belitt

Translations by Ben Belitt and
Alastair Reid

GROVE PRESS, INC. NEW YORK

For LILA BATH
and all our Mexicos
—B.B.

Some of these translations have appeared in the following periodicals:
The Bennington Review, Encounter (London), *Evergreen Review, Mundus Artium, The Nation, The New York Times Book Review, Poetry, The Southern Review,* and *Tri-Quarterly;* sections of the introductory essay
have appeared in *Mundo Nuevo* (Paris), *Mundus Artium, Razón y Fábula*
(Bogotá), *The Southern Review,* and *Voyages.*

Library of Congress Catalog Card Number: 68–58155

First Printing

Manufactured in the United States of America

Contents

Contents / v

vi / Contents

Contents / *vii*

Pablo Neruda: A New Decade
by
Ben Belitt

1. *The Laughing Neruda*

Criticism of Neruda both in this country and South America has paid long homage to the fact—a profound, rather than a peripheral one—that whoever touches his work, touches Chile; and that ultimately, whoever touches Chile touches the whole ambience of Spanish letters. With the passing of time, however, it has become clear that appraisal has languished as well as prospered on this account; for while the achievement of Pablo Neruda has gone on crossing boundaries and denying "establishments," comment has remained singularly narrow, inbred, and positional. Too often the effect has been to decant the total essence of a much displaced identity into a "Chilean Indian from Parral," chemically inseparable from the stones, the forests, and the coastal waters of his own country. Both his admirers and his detractors dwell obsessively on particulars of Chilean landscape or Chilean politics which diminish rather than enlarge an intransigent personal vision. Compiling a long index of place-names and public occasions, they have turned a poet's dispensation to the world into a family quarrel or a South American property.

To be sure, any program which includes the *Canto general de Chile, Las piedras de Chile,* and *Memorial de Isla Negra,* and teems with anecdote and personal history, requires a glossary for North American readers. An overlay of continents, jungles, rivers, cities, and oceans seems to cover Neruda's world like a cartographer's isinglass; and much of *La arena traicionada, Crónica de 1948,* and *Las oligarquías* will require the fine print of topical Hispanists to be wholly intelligible to readers in 1968. Nevertheless, it is a fact that the *Canto general de Chile* was ultimately absorbed into a *Canto general*, and, as the poet went on to explain: "Amidst all these visions, I wanted to paint a portrait of the struggles and victories of America as part of our very zoology and geology . . . It is a lyric attempt to confront our whole universe."[1] The true range of Pablo Neruda will never become apparent (especially to Swedish Academicians) until one has reckoned with explicit directives furnished us by his titles. His "lyric" mode embraces (1) songs (*Veinte poemas de amor y una canción desesperada*, 1924), (2) chants (*Canto general*, 1950, *Cantos ceremoniales*, 1960), (3) odes (three books of *Odas elementales*, 1954–1959), (4) sonnets (*Cien sonetos de amor*, 1959), (5) sonatas (*Sonata crítica*, 1964), and most recently (6) barcaroles (*La barcarola*, 1968). His range is "general," "elemental," "ceremonial," and "memorial," rather than topical; and his "residence," three times over, is "on earth" (*Residencia en la tierra, I, II, III*)— or when it is not on earth, it is airy, fiery, or oceanic.

A bibliography of Pablo Neruda guides us to these key terms as surely as it detains us en route in Punitaqui, Macchu Picchu, Spain, Asia, and Isla Negra. It is to these terms, as indices to the further range of Pablo Neruda, that I should like to address myself in an introduction intended, for once, not as a translator's primer for non-Hispanic readers, but as one poet's meditation on another. I shall assume, because his essential gravity in 1968 pulls the depths and meanings that way, that the poetry of Pablo Neruda is part of everything else I know and sense about work of genius everywhere; that it is not a special *barrio* or ghetto of the contemporary mind known only to the case worker and the Spanish-speaking expert in segregated mentalities; that we have wrangled too wastefully about public commitment and thought too little of the solitude of an interior stance; that his work, given "free and innocent passage," resonates against literatures other than his own, including the English, from which he

---

[1] Alfredo Cardona Peña, *Pablo Neruda y otros ensayos* (Mexico: Ediciones de Andrea, 1955), p. 40.

has translated Blake, Joyce, and Shakespeare,[2] and that this resonance is the true measure of his long traffic with the democracy of letters.

Any revaluation of the achievement of Pablo Neruda must, I think, pause for a long, second look at a volume published after four volumes of "odes" under the fanciful title of *Estravagario* in 1958, and apparently more important to Neruda than to his critics and countrymen. Partisans of Neruda's odic and "residential" manner, fellow travelers for whom the "only" book is *Rail-Splitter, Awake!*, gravid devotees of his *Twenty Love Poems,* and cultists of Macchu Picchu have all tended to set it aside as an interim work, like his youthful *Crepusculario* (1923)—which the oddity of its title may serve to recall. Precisely how to render the neologistic force of the title is a translator's problem which need not detain the reader for long. It is a word of prismatic obliquity, splitting the glancing illuminations of *extraviar*: to get lost, to wander off course, to divagate; *extravagante*: extravagant, eccentric, way out; *vagar*: to loiter or potter; and to English ears, at least, *vagary*, whimsy, caprice. If it is possible to call *Crepusculario* Neruda's *Book of Twilight* it may be permissible to call *Estravagario* his *Book of Vagaries.*

The titular linguistics are important only because an unplaceable word may also help to locate an unplaceable intonation and suggest the humors which invest it like an aura. The "unplaceable" factor is, indeed, something more than an aura: it is both a destination and a predicament. As "destination," its intent is to throw the complacent reader for whom Neruda is either a monolith or a public convenience, offcourse; and as a predicament, it offers a comic bath of "negative capability" in which the poet romps like a water weasel. On the one hand, his "delights are dolphin-like," and

---

[2]See *Visiones de las hijas de Albión y El viajero mental (Visions of the Daughters of Albion and The Mental Traveler) por William Blake* (Madrid: Cruz y Raya, 1934). Also republished by Ediciones Botella Al Mar, undated. His translation of *Romeo and Juliet* has recently been published by Editorial Losada, S. A., Buenos Aires, 1966, as No. 308 in their *Biblioteca clásica y contemporánea.*

"show his back above / The element they liv'd in": on the other, they toil in the "thick rotundity of the world" for the center of a poet's disturbance, groping for transparency. Neruda's avowed penchant for "impurity,"[3] however, constantly deflects him into private caprice, a *coquetería* of unanswered solicitations, digressions of the mind's finalities into the absurd, the quizzical, and the imponderable. With good reason, he enlists the "camp" of antiquarian steel engravings from an obsolete *Works of Jules Verne,* and the "pop" of a *Book of Illustrated Objects*[4] resembling a Sears-Roebuck for the Mexican provinces, printed in San Luis Potosí in 1883. Against this iconography of persiflage, savored by a mind that shrugs away all fictions of solution, including the political, Neruda enters his defense of ignorance as an aspect of the world's redeeming impurity.

The epistemology of ignorance is the constantly augmented theme in a work which might otherwise seem a packet of damp squibs, rather than the fuse to a spiritual explosion. It begins vaguely with a cluster of unexamined intuitions: "It is dark in the mothering earth / and dark within me"; "the whole world frightens me—death and cold water"; "I am tired of the hard sea and the mysterious earth," of old hens, bad *aperitifs,* good education, statues, of concessions, of "everything well-made" and "that ages us." Who would have surmised, asks Neruda, that "earth would change her old skin in so many ways?"—with an afterthought out of Wonderland itself: "We go falling down the well of everyone else." His best hunch brings him close to the anguish of his three *Residencias*: "We are crucially alone / I propose to ask questions / let's talk man-to-man . . . No one knows what he's talking about / but all agree it is urgent."

---

[3]"Sobre una poesía sin pureza," *Obras completas* (Buenos Aires: Editorial Losada, S. A., 1957), pp. 1822–23. Translated in *Selected Poems of Pablo Neruda,* tr. and ed. by Ben Belitt, Introduction by Luis Monguió (New York: Grove Press, 1961), pp. 39–40.

[4]See first edition of *Estravagario* as published by Editorial Losada (Buenos Aires, 1958). The adornments, profuse in the original edition, are omitted in the more recent *Obras completas,* Editorial Losada (1962) (1968).

Meanwhile, a sense of self-loss and the withering away of the known renders both question and answer increasingly remote. There is mockery as well as pathos in his clown's grimace: "My heart is so heavy / with the things that I know / it's like dragging / a dead weight of stones in a sack"; or "No matter how many we are or I am / at the moment / I can never meet up with a soul: they lose me under my clothing / they went off to some other city." At times a child's recalcitrance edges the irony of the poet's denial: "I'm not asking anyone anything / but every day I know less": "Why (do I) recognize nobody / and why does nobody recognize me?" The comedy of the amateur's stage fright, pinned down by spotlight and audience, does not escape him: "I don't know what to do with my hands / and I've thought of doing without them / —but how will I put on my ring? / What an awful uncertainty!" Sheepishly, quizzically, he calls out from his treadmill: "I don't come, I don't go / I don't dress, I don't walk about in the nude / I've thrown forks, / spoons and knives into the well. / I smile only at myself / I don't ask indiscreet questions." "Which is which, which is how?"

The true distress of the poet, however, is never far from his vagaries, and is frequently summed up in a cry: "What must I do to sort myself out? / How can I provide for myself?" The hazards of the absurd show their darkened as well as their lighted side: "A shadow moves over the earth / man's spirit is shadow / and therefore it moves." There are admonitions, cautionary asides: "I don't want to mislead myself again / it is dangerous to walk / backward, because all at once / the past is a prison." In stroboscopic changes of dark and light the poet can only assure others grimly: "From time to time, at a certain remove, / one must take one's bath in a grave"; and himself: "I'm going to open and close myself up / with my most treacherous friend, / Pablo Neruda."

The result is a parody of Socratic quest in which Neruda, committed to the "clarification of things," puts his question to priest, physician, gravedigger, and "specialists in cremation," in turn. No one will miss, under his shifting humors, macabre and impudent by turns, the shock of the poet's concussion with Death, like a roadblock barring the way to the motorist turning a curve at top speed: "The minute vanishes, vanishes over one's shoulder," and "suddenly we have only one year to move on / a month, a day, and death touches our calendar." The responses, as I have tried to suggest, are riddlingly diverse, from the child's game of hide-and-seek: "Let's count up to twelve now / Then: everyone—quiet!", to the radiologist's glare: "Everyone sees / the plight of my shocked viscera / in radioterrible pictures," to spiritual panic: "Help! Help! Give us a hand! / Help us to be earthier day after day! / Help us to be / holier spray, / come airier out of the wave!" Since finalities and outcomes are hardly germane to a *Book of Vagaries*, the answer remains sybilline to the end: "When the wind skims / your skull's hollows / it will show you enigmas / whispering the truth / where your ears used to be." His ultimate impersonations are perhaps three: "I am a teacher of life / and a vague student of death"; "I am one who lives / in mid-ocean, close to twilight / and further away than these stones"; "I am he who makes dreams; / in my house of feather and stone / with a knife and a clock / I cut clouds and waves / and out of these elements / I contrive my calligraphy."

The significance of this glancing look backward at Neruda's book of vagaries may not yet be apparent to the casual reader. It is, in the literal sense of the word, a pivotal book: it veers away sharply, like that "swimmer of heaven" in his concluding Testament, from the resolute materiality of his odes and "general songs," and "leaps into transparency." Certain only that "those who would give me advice / become crazier with each passing day"—including the "politically astute" who note down all deviations, who "wrinkle, grow gray, and can't stomach their chestnuts," our hero of comic impurity, like the celebrated squire from La Mancha, retires to take counsel. In full sight of the utopian dream and the "sad countenance" of his master, he parodies his predicament with the country humors of a yokel: "Now I don't know which way to be— / absent-minded or respectful; / shall I yield to advice / or tell them outright they're hysterical? / Independence, it's clear, gets me nowhere. / I get lost in the underbrush / I don't know if I'm coming or go-ing. / Shall I take off, or stand firm, / pay for tomcats or tomatoes?" His decision, in the owlish "Parthenogenesis," is stubborn, circular, and mocking: "I'll figure out as best I can / what I ought *not* to do—and then do it . . . If I don't make mistakes / who will believe in my errors? . . . I'll change my whole person / . . . and then when I'm different / and no one can recognize me / I'll keep doing the same things that I did / since I couldn't possibly do otherwise."

Apart from the immediate drolleries of this soliloquy, which in effect returns a rebellious Sancho Panza to the serv-ice of a dream, there would be some somber things to say. Philosophically, it poses questions regarding the nature and uses of "advice" as a species of knowledge, about the valid-ity of the "independent" stance as a clue to autonomous reality, about standing firm, moving off, and tactical error as a test of identity, about the changeable, the innate, and the learned. All are recognizably "existential" preoccupations, all are recklessly and joyously engaged in page after page of the *Estravagario*.

In this sense, Neruda at times comes close to the mood of his younger countryman, Nicanor Parra, with whose "anti-poems" the harlequinade of *Estravagario* has often been as-sociated by South American critics. Certainly, it would be a mistake to overlook the affinities of the two major talents of Chile who in 1958—the year of the publication of *La Cueca Larga* and *Estravagario*—undertook to scrutinize each other at length in an exchange of *Discursos* concerned with the criteria and intent of poetry in a new decade of the South American idiom. It would be equally misleading to overlook the fact that the "anti-poem" was *always* present in the pro-tean repertory of Pablo Neruda, in poems such as "Walking Around," from the *Residencias*, in the hard-bitten reportage of *Canto general* and the witty emaciations of the *Odas*; and that, indeed, the whole premise of an "impure" poetry in-voked by Neruda in 1935 is the true precursor of the "anti-poem" both in Nicanor Parra and South American letters as a whole. The "anti-poem," after all, is an importation and not an invention of Parra's: it predates the *Poemas y anti-*

poemas in the work of Corbière, Apollinaire, Pound, Eliot, Cummings and Brecht, among others, and has been endlessly adumbrated in a genre of "anti-plays," "anti-novels," "anti-worlds," "non-essays," et cetera, which bear witness to the deflationary trend of the modern imagination in the service of the ignoble, the apostate, and the absurd. In purely Hispanic terms, it is written into the whole of *Don Quixote* where, as another avowed enemy of the baroque, Antonio Machado, liked to point out, the "Cervantine fiction" or anti-romance, calls for a "double time" and a "double space," a "twinned series of figures—real and hallucinatory . . . two integral complementary consciousnesses conversing and forging ahead" in a "book of harlequinade creating a spiritual climate which is ours to this day."

It is equally proper to suppose that the poems of *Estravagario* represent, politically, a kind of "revisionism" by a servant of good will, in the aftermath of extraordinary devotion to party lines, dogmas, tactics, and disciplines. In this case, the disengagements of *Estravagario* show both the irreverence and autonomy of Neruda's commitment to an ideology. Consulting the Presidium of his own pulses, testing the "equivocal cut of my song," he discovers he is no man's Establishment ("rector of nothing"), and in the realignment of checks and balances, opens the way to a decade of unprecedented self-scrutiny. It is to this later decade that we now turn.

2. *A House of Fourteen Planks*

Despite the prominence given it in the title and the body of the sonnets themselves, the key word of Neruda's *One Hundred Love Sonnets* (*Cien sonetos de amor, 1959*) is not "love" but "clarity" (*claridad*). The almost Parnassian abstraction of the term may jog some startled memories of the "très-chère," "très-belle / Qui remplit mon coeur de clarté" of Baudelaire,[5] with his equally troubled dream of a voyage

---

[5]"Hymne," *Oeuvres complètes* (Paris: Bibliothèque de la Pléiade, Librairie Gallimard, 1954), p. 222.

under "wet suns" and "disheveled skies" to consummations where *"tout n'est qu'ordre et beauté."*[6] It is significant that, in the protean world of tidal impulses, oceanic disorder, diurnal and seasonal change which shapes the progressions of the Sonnets—Neruda's characteristic insistence upon the impurities of function and the unfolding telluric and human improvisations of a lifetime—it is *claridad* that the poet has come to espouse, literally, in the person of the Beloved.

The more closely one follows the word through the poet's calendar of "morning, afternoon, evening, and night" with its intimations of changing seasons glimpsed through the "salt disaster" of water, the "mash of the light," "all that shudders below / underfoot, underground," "the insubstantial fog," "an untimely autumn," "today, tomorrow, yesterday" that "destroy themselves in passing," the more one comes to feel its spiritual rather than its cerebral force in the poem. Only occasionally does it connect with the world of quantitative and syllogistic order, as when, viewing the Southern Cross through the "night of the human," Neruda invokes its "four zodiacal numbers" in an image of cosmological serenity. Even here, the numbers and elements connect "for a passing minute only"; the "green cross" is straightway vegetalized into parsley, animalized into fish and firefly, carbonized into diamond, absorbed into the chemistry of fermenting wine.

However imperfectly seen, however, it is the *claridad* of Matilde Urrutia which constitutes the poet's vision of love's permanence and the world's changes. It is Neruda's word for the beautiful just as *integritas, consonantia, claritas* came to constitute a triad of spiritual properties of the beautiful for St. Thomas; with the special anguish of Neruda's passion for the secular way. On one hand we have the "waves' shock on unconsenting stone," "the seaweed's sodden aroma," "the towering spumes of Isla Negra"; on the other, we have the "dear Orderer" (*Ordenadora*) who "thrust[s] herself into the subterranean world," bringing definition, the "order [that] apportions its dove and its daily bread": recognizably sacramental images of providence and redemption. In be-

[6]*Ibid.,* "L'Invitation au Voyage," p. 127.

tween, moves the "flying hand" of the housewife, arranging cups, saucers, casseroles, "walking or running, singing or planting, sewing or cooking or nailing things down / writing, returning": and in the realm of brute nature, the tides, the breakers, the "ocean's tormented pavilions," the "machinations of the wasp / who toils in behalf of a universe of honey," and the poet's "leaky barge adrift / within a double skyline: dream and order."

The latent "religiosity" of crosses, doves, bread, wine, honey, the "crown of knives," the "scarecrow smiling his bloody smile," "mockers and backbiters," merits some passing notice, despite Neruda's wry disavowal of any "plaiting and peddling of thorns." If the doves of Sonnet LXXVIII have more in common with the doves painted by Picasso for the Second Congress of the Defenders of Peace, and the bread is the bread written into the traditional slogans of proletarian revolt from the French Commune to the Petrograd uprisings of 1917, the special *claridad* of the Sonnets makes them resonate freshly against universal archetypes which have attended the strivings of the spirit in all ages. It is no disservice to the hard-won contemporaneity of Neruda to point out that his mystique of an "impure poetry" for engaged poets everywhere has Christian as well as existential overtones in its insistence on a "corruptible" state upon which imaginative transcendence depends. The impure, the fallen, the perishing, all that "escapes the interstices" when the net of human order has been knotted by the rational orderer, dominate the watery brooding of Neruda throughout the whole of the poet's later *oeuvre*, since the *Estravagario*.

The task of the *Cien sonetos de amor* is to retrieve an "immaculate day" in all the temporal impurity of its hours, phases, seasons, alternations of feeling and light, fixed in the last, happy *claritas* of love. On the compositional level, the labor begins with a "profanation" of the sonnet form itself, which, despite its careful count of fourteen lines apiece, omits both the end rhymes and the metrical profile which dynamize the "sonnetification" of feeling and argument, and leaves the thought to work its way through tercets and quatrains as an act of nature. Indeed, it is Neruda's intent, according to his dedicatory note to the light-and-dark lady of his sonnets, to turn the sonnet form itself *wooden*. "In proposing such a project for myself," he writes, "I was well aware that, along the edges of each [sonnet], by deliberate preference and for purpose of elegance, poets in every age have set rhymes to ring out like silver or crystal or cannon shot. In all humility, I have made these sonnets out of wood, given them the sound of that opaque and pure substance, and they should be so heard by your ears. You and I, walking through forests and sand wastes, by lost lakes and cindery latitudes, gathered those splinters of pure timber, beams delivered to the inconstancy of the water and weather. Out of the very smoothest fragments of all I have fashioned, with hatchet, penknife, and cold steel, these lumberyards of love and raised little houses of fourteen planks where your eyes, so sung and adored, may live on."

The seasoned reader of Neruda, aware of the poet's long apotheosis of wood as an image of the strenuous materiality of the world's body, will know how to make the most of this courtly compliment. The poet of the Araucanian forests who wrote:

> Whatever it is that I know
> or invoke again,
> among all the things of the world,
> it is wood that abides
> as my playfellow,
> I take through the world
> in my flesh and my clothing
> the smell
> of the sawyer,
> the reek of red boards . . .

proffers his "lumberyard of love" as confidently as sonneteers of the past have come with their more traditional nosegays and proud disavowals of marble and gilded monuments: the realism of Neruda is not pejorative. It is, however, "impure." His "century of wooden sonnets," while retaining the classical count of Quevedo and Góngora and addressing itself to themes as Petrarchan as the prosody they espouse, keep open-ended, like a paragraph of prose. Read against the tailored profiles of his great predecessors, the shagginess and waywardness of his sonnets are constantly apparent. They contract at will to the minimal beat of

Trājo ēl amōr su cōla de dolōres

or spring open like a sonnet by Gerard Manley Hopkins:

Nō sōlo por las tiērras desiērtas dōnde la piēdra salīna

from one sonnet to the next. As little "houses of fourteen planks" unfenestrated by end rhyme, they remain resolutely functional and unadorned: they house only large movements of the mind and show the grain and the knot of the poet's intention, rather than gargoyles of the prosodist's virtuosity.

On the other hand, it would be a mistake to assume that they comprise a landscape of blockhouses and framed plank, like those pioneering encampments of the poet's childhood which went up in periodic holocausts and were rebuilt by Temucans "who know how to build in a hurry." Viewed against the profile of the wonderfully spindled and granulated *Odes*—or indeed, from any vantage point along the circumference of poetry as such—his "century of sonnets" registers with remarkable elegance as a city of the mind in which passion and meditation come and go with powerful strides toward a noble objective. Indeed, it is with something of surprise that one comes to realize—as an afterthought, rather than a concession to the "rail-splitting" Neruda—that the customary stabilizers and parquetry of sonnet are not regularly present in the unfolding poem. This is due, in part, to the "feminine" genius of latinate discourse as such, with its functional repetition of identical or assonantal slack syllables which makes it almost impossible, at least to Anglo-Saxon ears, for Italian and Spanish not to *seem* to rhyme.

Closer reading reveals, however, the deeply traditional source of both the eloquence and the concord of the *Sonnets*.

The density of a quatrain like the following, for example, should be apparent even without the translator's gloss:

Ay de mí, ay de nosotros, bienamada,
sólo quisimos sólo amor, amarnos,
y entre tantos dolores se dispuso
sólo nosotros dos ser malheridos.

The eloquence is there because the elegance is there, the traditional rhetoric of invocation and lament balancing romantic outcry with Gongoristic refinement, parallel syncopation of key words: *sólo, nosotros, amada, amarnos.* In Sonnet LXVI, where all is sparely set on the bones of the sonnet, and end rhyme is regular, Neruda proves that he can, at will, produce a sonnet in the vein of the Spanish masters, where the combining elements—marked density, parallelism, repetition, and a "Shakespearean" prosody so adroitly fused with the "Italianate" as to create a continuous texture of two end rhymes used six and eight times respectively—all point the way to the sources in Quevedo and Góngora so highly esteemed by the poet.

On the whole, the effect of Neruda's constant *suavización* of the lines is to exchange the whittler's "penknife" for the eloquence of the cabinetmaker and the artisan. The fact that the eloquence is virile, flexible, intimate, need deceive no one, just as his earlier identification with Lincoln as railsplitter (*El Leñador*) and Vallejo as "carpenters, poor carpenters," is inseparable from his compositional integrities as an artist. The *Cien sonetos de amor* are a landmark in the literature of the sonnet that confirms again the catholicity of Neruda's genius at its flood tide, at the same time that it breathes new life into dry sticks. It acomplishes the miracle of transforming that most servile and feudal of forms—the sonnet's long complaint of knightly self-denial and court compliment contrived for the express delectation of a patron —into a husband's book of hours, grievances, privacies, troubled meditations. It removes the inamorata, once coy and cruel by turns, from her medieval tower, into the kitchen, with its recognizably bourgeois panoply of "cups and glasses

/ cruets of oil and oleaginous golds," sets her, sharp as a snapshot, against a background of "blue salt, with the sun on the breakers," as she emerges, "mother-naked . . . taking her place in the world." It eternizes her in "ovens of clay with Temuco adobe," without the Renaissance boast of indestructibility for "this scribbling on the paper." In its fusion of both the elegant and the immediate, it proves again the eventual sophistication of Neruda's premise of the Impure as a species of "pastoral," in which, as Empson once pointed out, the complex man goes to school to the simple man "to mirror more completely the effective elements of the society he lived in."[7]

3. The Mourning Neruda

The year 1961–1962 is notable, in Neruda's long chronicle of plenty, for the publication of three volumes of verse, each differing from the other in form and subject matter, and all in marked contrast to the special rigors of the *Sonnets*: *Las piedras de Chile* (*The Stones of Chile*), *Cantos ceremoniales* (*Ceremonial Songs*), and *Plenos poderes* (*Full Powers*). *The Stones of Chile*, which the poet with good reason calls his "flinty book," not only follows the format of a volume by Pierre Seghers celebrating the stones of France, with photographs by Antonio Quintana, but, we are told in a preface, was "twenty years in my mind." During those years, Neruda contemplated the coastland of Chile with its "portentous presences in stone," which he later transformed "into a hoarse and soaking language, a jumble of watery cries and primordial intimations." The result is a "memorial" which organizes Neruda's lifelong fascination with the craggy, the telluric, and the metallurgical into a veritable Stonehenge of exact and monumental fantasy. The dimensions and intensities shift from poem to poem and image to image, from gigantic evocations in the vein of his *Macchu Picchu*, to

---

[7] I: "Proletarian Literature," William Empson, *English Pastoral Poetry* (New York: W. W. Norton and Co., 1938), p. 12.

pebbles for the passing delight of a child, to memorial cairns and barrows elegizing the metamorphoses and convulsions of geological time. This is no mere programmatic picture book of curiosities, however, ready-made for the sightseer— no tourist's guide to the stones of Chile as "house," "harp," "hairy ship," "big table," or a bestiary of playful petrefactions including a bull, an ox, a lion, a turtle, and three ducklings. It is a freehand lithography of time and the spirit.

In any other hands, *The Stones of Chile* might well have turned into a marginal rather than a residual book, a mineralized eschatology. What is remarkable is the speed and the certainty with which Neruda, working in sportive and approximate contexts—the profiles which distance and illusion confer on stones—divines a deeper subject twenty years in the making, like antediluvian artifacts in the "corings" of a geologist. The poet's *aficiones* for wood, water, cereals, stars, shells, are already well-known staples of his substantive world, manifestations of his deep purchase on the "impure." His essay on "oceanography,"[8] with its spacy trajectory from the Pillars of Hercules to the *krakens* of Copenhagen and the *narwhals* of the North Sea, his conchologist's passion for the artifacts of the sea floor, his delight in plankton and the sea horse (rendered doubly attractive by the Spaniard's whimsical equivalence: *"unicornio marino"*) similarly confirm his passion for the oceanic. *The Stones of Chile* takes a titan's step forward to fix them all in a massive *assemblage* of images, Medusan in its genius for turning to stone all it gazes upon.

The result, curiously enough, is not frozen Heraclitus or stopwatched Bergson, but a set of poems which yield to the imagination at every turn: which breathes, dissolves, nourishes like those visceral deposits secreted by the ambergris whale so often observed by the poet from his Isla Negra window.[9] Nothing is less static or earthbound than the stones

---

[8]"Oceanografía dispersa," *Obras completas* (Buenos Aires: Editorial Losada, S. A., 1957), pp. 1825–27.

[9]*Ibid.*, p. 1825: "In this way, the green whale (*Bachianetas glaucus*), enroute to the South Pacific and the warm islands facing my windows in Isla Negra, gets his nourishment."

of Neruda's Chile: by his "Great Rock Table" the "child that is truth in a dream / and the faith of the earth" waits "for his portion"; in his Harp, nothing moves but "a world's lonely music / congealing and plunging and trying its changes"; his Ship sails placelessly through deaths and distances; and out of his Blind Statue, he "cut[s] through the stone / of my joy toward . . . the effigy shaped like myself," devising "hands, fingers, eyes." Caliban's world of rock and primordial ooze is transformed into Ariel's domain of light, speed, scintillations, island music, ether:

> In the stripped stone
> and the hairs of my head
> airs move
> from the rock and the wave.
> Hour after hour, that changing of skins,
> the salt in the light's marination.

Despite the frequently "hoarse and soaking language," the "jumble of watery cries and primordial intimations," the impact of the volume is neither sodden nor wooden. Its contour remains, as it should, sculptural, mobile, diaphanous: "weddings of time and the amethyst," "marriages of snow and the sea" which mirror "the heart's whole transparency / in / the boulder / the water."

By contrast, the *Ceremonial Songs*, also dated 1961, is a more diverse work than either the book of sonnets or the book of stones. The title at once directs us to a difference of tempo, scale, intonation. In opting for the "ceremonial," certainly, Neruda is removing himself from the "general"—a designation he was happy to claim for that heroic compendium embracing fifteen volumes and 568 pages in the original edition published in 1950 (*Canto general*). Since the poet himself does not dwell on the "ceremonial" factor as such, one is left to deduce its attributes from a scrutiny of the constituent songs: their content, their form, the whole ambience of the "ceremonious" inflection. One notes, first of all, that it is a book which deals in sequences, concatenations, trains of poems, rather than "taciturn castles"[10] of stone or "little houses of fourteen planks":[11] it is a book of long poems—the longest in twenty-two sections and the shortest in four—of a decidedly meditative and exploratory cast. The subjects fall readily into four general categories: commemorative pieces devoted to literary and historical personages (Manuela Sáenz, lover of Simon Bolívar; de Lautréamont); seasonal pieces, embracing midsummer and the rainy season; landscapes (Spain, Cadiz, the cordilleras of Chile, the ocean); and introspective pieces like "Cataclysm" and "Party's End," in which the poet contemplates his world, his person, and his scruples with a characteristic rotation or circuition of the troubled matters it contemplates.

The range of *Ceremonial Songs*, then, is ambitious: there is no attempt on the poet's part to mitigate the gravity and duration of his inductive labors. On the contrary, it seems to be one of the shaping criteria of the "ceremonial" that it aggrandizes and solemnizes whatever it touches. To be "ceremonious," apparently, is to be formal, speculative, unhurried: to build more and more *time* into the unfolding of the mind's apprehension of itself. In the realm of content, it is also, clearly, to celebrate and to elegize. However diversely the subject veers from persons to places, and from places to the things which embody them, the unity of mood, temper, tone, throughout the *Ceremonial Songs*—a kind of spiritual seepage—remains inviolable to the end.

At first reading, the persisting factor is felt to be a pervasive melancholy; but successive rereadings fix the melancholy as profoundly elegiac in origin. Only by adding the elegiac weight of the *Ceremonial Songs* to the cosmic and erotic melancholy of the sonnets and the book of stones, can one begin to intimate the distinguishing cachet of the later poetry of Pablo Neruda. What remains to be noted in the whole vista of the late Neruda, from its whimsical inklings in *Estravagario* to the processional densities of *La Bar-*

---

[10]*Ibid.*, "Algunas palabras para este libro de piedras," p. 1717. A whimsical allusion to the poems in *The Stones of Chile.*

[11]*Ibid.*, "A Matilde Urrutia," p. 1649. The "little houses" are, of course, the sonnets of *One Hundred Love Sonnets.*

carola,[12] is the *de-ideologizing* of his subject and its nervy containment in immediate acts of the poet's mind: his increasing reluctance to terminate existing doubts by rational acts of the will. It is this that imparts to all the hopes, apprehensions, positional assurances of the poet, their penumbral melancholy. And it becomes the task of "ceremony" to mediate between melancholia and the world, summoning up what is left of the old dispensation and casting out despair by re-imagining the real in existential rather than ideological terms.

In short, the "ceremonial" songs serve notice that we have to do with a *mourning* Neruda, a *"poeta enlutado"*: not in the pusillanimous guise which Neruda rejects both for himself and a perishing world ("The stones do not mope!") but the mourning once deemed "becoming" to Elektra, orphaned exemplar of the world's kinship. Certainly it would be a disservice to suggest that the "mourning Neruda," like the "music-practising Socrates,"[13] is not sustained and consoled at every turn by political particulars which, in the striker's militant parlance of the 30's, *organize* in the midst of mourning. Indeed, nothing is more apparent in the spectrum of Neruda's labors as poet and humanist than the energizing genius of both his melancholy and his empirical anguish. On the other hand, the abiding presence of the *poeta enlutado*— to which he testifies everywhere without guile or reservation —is equally apparent as a constant of his imaginative sensibility. If, in 1924, he begins with a ratio of "twenty love poems" to "one desperate song" (*Veinte poemas de amor y una canción desesperada*), the evidence of his work throughout the three *Residencias* makes it clear that the desperate song was actually unending, and determined the "surrealis-

---

[12]Work in progress, of which a fragment, entitled *"Amores: Matilde"* appears in Volume V (*Sonata crítica*) of *Memorial de Isla Negra*. Further "fragments" appear in a pamphlet published by Ediciones de la Rama Florida (Lima: 1966), in an edition limited to 300 numbered copies. The volume itself was published in December 1967 by Editorial Losada (Buenos Aires).

[13]Friedrich Nietzsche, *The Birth of Tragedy,* tr. Francis Golffing (Garden City: Doubleday Anchor, 1956), p. 90.

tic" displacements wrought by his prerevolutionary acedia. ("It so happens I'm tired of just being a man.") And if, as Luis Monguió has suggested,[14] the emergent politics of Neruda turns the world's melancholy into a celebration in which "*every* song is a love song," the seminal reciprocities of love and melancholy remain significant.

A sampling of the progressions of the most ingratiating of the pieces will serve to illustrate both the tactics and the dynamics of the "ceremonial": *Fin de fiesta / Party's End*— the terminal book of the poem as a whole. To all intents and purposes, the occasion of this vortical poem in thirteen parts is scenic and seasonal: the "first rains of March," the seacoasts of Isla Negra, and the omnipresent changes of the Ocean. Underneath this amalgam, however, like a tidal force under a breaker, a deeper theme asserts itself: the confrontation of renewable nature with unrenewable man. It manifests itself first in the motif which gives the poem its ironically lackadaisical title: the theme of "*fiesta.*" By "fiesta," it appears, Neruda intends the gregarious drive that assembles, celebrates, and eventually disperses all things—not merely the single "reveler," but the corporate being of his "words and mouths," the "roads" by which he materializes and disappears. By Section Two, the poet has accomplished a kind of symbiotic fusion of the Season, the Man, and the Festival, into a single aspect of the world's temporality.

The motifs of seasonal rain and the sea return in Section Three, "exploding in salt," ebbing, delaying, "leaving only a glare on the sea," and are churned into a "spray" of eschatological wonderment. On the one hand, the "submerged things" of the universe ask: "Where are we going?" and on the other, the algae riding the currents ask: "What am I?" They are answered by "wave after wave after wave," with Heraclitean enigmas: "One rhythm creates and destroys and continues: / truth lies in the bitter mobility."

The word "bitter" ("*amargo*") is a clue to the encompassing melancholy that thereafter seeps into the matrix of the

---

[14]*Selected Poems of Pablo Neruda*, tr. and ed. by Ben Belitt, Introduction by Luis Monguió (New York: Grove Press, 1961), p. 29.

piece and turns all into an elegiac meditation on the efficacy of human exertion—the people, footprints, dead papers, "transportation expenses" (*"gastos de transportes"*) of man's efforts to match the unkillable being of the world with acts of the will and imagination. Here the weariness of the poet is such that he asks for a suspension, if not indeed a liquidation, of the inhabited world: inhabited poems, inhabited beaches, inhabited time, where the "habitable" is construed as the "distinguishing mark" of individual initiative: "for a moment let no living creature enter my verse." For the first time since the *Residencias* of his youth, Neruda, looking away from causes, factions, ideological commitments, into the void where the crystal expands, the rocks climb the silence, and the ocean "destroys itself," restates that heresy of all engaged protagonists: "It so happens I'm tired of just being a man." A more haunting issue, apparently, has presented itself with his returning acedia: it is the "marring of energy," and the miracle by which "the ocean destroys itself without marring its energy." The quantitative anguish of things is summed up by Neruda in another outcry, which measures the inadequacy of a world in which "our fathers in patches and hand-me-downs . . . entered the warehouses as one entered a terrible temple": the consumer's outcry of *How much?*

Thus, a third of the way into a shifting and many-sided poem, the backlash of baffled intentionality reasserts itself in political and polemical terms. A new insistence on expedient protestation—on "the whithers and wherefores / wherever it pleases me—from the throne to the oil-slick / that bloodies the world," mounting as the "grains of my anger grew greater," turns the purchaser's *How much?* into the prophet's and the revolutionary's *How long?* There follows another turn of the poet's imagination as a new assault of personal choice on the inequalities of the human condition flows into the voids and pockets of his initial melancholy. It is this systole-diastole of his meditative patterns that is the distinctive mark of the "mourning and organizing" Neruda. Indeed, he seems to breathe like a sponge on the ocean floor of his exacerbated discomfiture. He absorbs doubts, contradictions, passing flotsam in the great baths of ricocheting images and uneasy afterthoughts which he inhabits, rocking in the play of altering pressures, volumes, thermal densities, speeds. No one has written more vividly than Neruda of the thermodynamics and psychology of the deep-sea diver (See "Ode to A Diver"[15]); and somewhere, at the critical depths which break or sustain the human violator of the oceanic and the subterranean, Neruda has known how to place the rational balances which turn chaos into meditative order.

The result is an elegiac poem not unlike the *Elegien* of Rilke in both the discontinuities of its empirical search for hard answers, its preoccupation with "the dead with the delicate faces," the "preciously dead,"[16] and its insistence on "clarity," joy, a strenuous humanism which asks nothing of "angels" in its pursuit of the heart's fears and the spirit's intimations. It differs from Rilke's "ceremonial" amalgam of melancholy, skepticism, and temporal love, of course, in its *visceralization* of thought—its commingling of thought with "the thorn's languages / the bite of the obdurate fish / the chill of the latitudes / the blood on the coral / the night of the whale"—and its pendulum backswing toward "men." The *"Engel-nicht–Menschen-nicht"* ("Not men, not angels"[17]) of Rilke's impasse, glimpsed only briefly in Section Four, is promptly exchanged for "the brutal imperative . . . that makes warriors of us, gives us the stance / and inflection of fighters," as Neruda crosses his "bridge of commitment" (*lo que hicimos*) into the "pride of a lifetime" and its "organized splendor" (*el esplandor organizado*).

If the accomplishment of Neruda in *Party's End*, however, were merely tactical and ideological, one might well prefer to sweep backward to the derogated Rilke for truer confrontations of the human condition. The triumph of *Party's End*, however, is that its oceanic circuits stay nowhere for long,

---

[15]*Ibid.,* pp. 226–233.

[16]Cf. Neruda's *"Los muertos de rostro tierno," "Los más amados muertos,"* with Rilke's *"den jugendlich Toten" (Die Sechste Elegie)* and the dead lovers of *Die Erste Elegie.*

[17]"First Elegy," Rainer Maria Rilke, *Duino Elegies,* tr. Stephen Spender (New York: W. W. Norton, 1939), p. 20.

are not positional. The day sought by Neruda, in the end, is neither paradisiac nor ideological: it is an "expendable day," "a day bringing oranges," rather than a day of reckoning— though some hint of the social dream clings to the after-thought: "the day / that is ours if we are there to retrieve it again." At the close of the poem, the "white spindrift," the "ungratified cup of the sky," the "watery autumn" move in again, and with them, the obdurate mobilities of a poet who remains "just as I was / with my doubts, with my debts, / with my loves / having a whole sea to myself." Apparently, it has been enough to "come back," to touch his "palms to the land," to "have built what I could / out of natural stone, like a native, open-handed," to "have worked with my rea-son, unreason, my caprices, / my fury and poise." No longer "deracinate" (*sin mis raices*) as man, as poet, as Chilean, clouded and luminous by turns, Neruda can now

> . . . say: "Here is my place," stripping myself down in
>   the light
> and dropping my hands in the sea,
> until all is transparent again
> there under the earth, and my sleep can be tranquil.

This redistillation of serenity clings to the whole of Neruda's *Plenos poderes* (1962), imparting to each of the thirty-six poems that unmistakable "fullness of power" to which its title bears witness. Weary "neither of being nor of nonbeing," still "puzzling over origins," professing his old "debts to min-erality," yet wavering "as between two lost channels under water," the poet "forges keys," "looks for locks," opens "broken doors," pierces "windows out to living." What was plaintive or suspended in the *Ceremonial Songs* brightens in the up-beat of re-examined commitment, for which Neruda's distinguishing word is *"deberes"*: obligations, and its ancil-lary variations in *deber*: ought, should, must, owe. Thus, in the introductory poem entitled *"Deberes del poeta"* ("The Poet's Obligations"), his concern is less with possibility than with necessity—the imperatives freely imagined and pro-fessed by the poet, to which Yeats gave the name of "responsibilities." The options subsumed under the "responsible" are at once explicit and mysterious: "I must hear and preserve without respite / the watery lament of my consciousness," "I must feel the blow of hard water / and gather it back in a cup of eternity," "I must encounter the absent," I must tell, I must leave, journey, protect, become, be, eat, and possess. Elsewhere, the poet alludes to the "responsibility of the minute hand," the accumulation of "persons and chores," "the imperious necessity for vigilance," "lonely sweetnesses and obligations," "mineral obligations," and "obligations intact in the spume." These, the poet explains, are compelled upon him "not by law or caprice, / but by chains: / each new way was a chain"; he calls for "caution: let us guard the order of this ode," but his mood is blithe: "I am happy with the mountainous debts / I took on . . . the rigid demand on myself of watchfulness / the impulse to stay myself, myself alone . . . my life has been / a singing between chance and resiliency."

Side by side with the theme of resiliency (*la dureza, la dura realidad*), goes a theme of *pureza*, purity, as both a measure of the poet's effectiveness and a reward of his happy "obligation." A table of variations would include not only a multitude of passing allusions—pure waves, pure lines, pure towers, pure waters, pure bodies, pure hearts, pure feet, pure salts—and their variants in *claro* (clear lessons, clear capitals, clear vigilance, as well as "clarities" that are smiling, cruel, and erect) but entire poems like *"Para lavar a un niño"* ("To Wash A Child") and *"Oda para planchar"* ("In Praise of Ironing"). All, says the poet, must be cleansed, washed, whitened, made clear: as in a Keatsian dream of "pure ablution round earth's human shores,"[18] the land's outline is washed by the salt (*sal que lava la línea*) and the land's edge washes the world (*La línea lava el mundo*). Not only does Neruda invoke "a time to walk clean" in the name of the newly washed infant, and insist on "ironing out" the whiteness of the sea itself (*hay que planchar el mar de su*

---

[18]Sonnet XX, *The Poetical Works of John Keats,* edited by H. W. Garrod (New York, London, Toronto: Oxford University Press, 1956), p. 372.

blancura); in the end poetry itself is made white: (*la poesía es blanca*).

Thus, between *dureza* and *pureza* (resiliency and purity) and *deberes* and *poderes* (obligations and powers) the poet "writes [his] book about what I am" (*escribo un libro de lo que soy*) with stunning mastery of all the themes which embody a total identity. The "mourning carpenter" (*enlutado carpintero*) of *Estravagario* and the *Sonnets* is still there, "attending the casket, tearless, / someone who stayed nameless to the end / and called himself metal or wood": he contributes two of the volume's eulogies, one addressed to the dead "C.O.S.C." and the other, to the nine-and-a-half-year old "little astronaut" whose "burning car" touches "Aldabaran, mysterious stone," and "crosses a life line." The old preoccupations with the lost and remembered of a poet bemused by the sacramental character of all change are found again in poems like "The Past" (*"Pasado"*); and the old melancholy ("To Sorrow," *"A la tristeza"*): "For a minute, for / a short life, / take away my light and leave me / to realize / my misery, my alienation." So, too, are the dead, "the poor dead" (*al difunto pobre*), the people (*el pueblo*), the nights and the flora of Isla Negra (*Alstromoería, la noche de Isla Negra*), farewells (*adioses*), births (*los nacimientos*), ocean, water, sea, planet, tower, bird—each lending new force to that fullness of power by virtue of which a master of chiaroscuro "in the full light of day" paradoxically still "walks in the shade."

4. *The Burning Sarcophagus*

The great watershed of the last decade of Pablo Neruda—the work which, at the present writing, soars like the terminal pylon of a bridge spanning four epochs including the *Residencias, Canto general,* and the *Odas*—is, of course, the Black Island Memorial (*Memorial de Isla Negra*), published in 1964 to solemnize the poet's sixtieth birthday. In effect, it constitutes a fourth gargantuan span over which flows the spiritual traffic of more than half a century, on its way to destinations as hazardous and uncharted as those previously inhabited by a poet who warns us:

> I have never set foot in the countries I lived in,
> every port was a port of return:
> I have no post cards, no keepsakes of hair
> from important cathedrals.

Its trajectory supports the weight, the diversity, and the architectural stresses of everything encountered en route: exile, deracination, embattled ideologies, and the vested enmity of the world. All that the poet has written, imagined, foresuffered in purgatorial changes of forms and allegiances: shapes of the "crepuscular," the erotic, the tentative, the "enthusiastic," halfway houses of wood and stone, and "residences" that metamorphose into bloody bivouacs in Spain, consulates in Rangoon, Ceylon, India, Mexico, France, flights into Russia, China, Mexico, Peru, "voyages and homecomings" to his native cordilleras—all the wanderings of Ishmael and The Prodigal Son, debouch like a great estuary into the pages of *Black Island Memorial*, from whose terminus "Casa La Chascona,"[19] a poet's "house of dishevelment," arises like a hand-hewn Acropolis.

One puts the case a little grandly because the poet's conception is almost orientally pyramidal in its vision of a monument built by the living for a residence *not* of this earth, as well as on it. *Black Island Memorial* is a chieftain's or a pharaoh's personal cenotaph, calling to mind the *alcazares* of Andalucía and the Heorots of Anglo-Saxon myth, hung with shields, talismans, shaggy animal pelts and precious stones, whalebone curiosities of the "seafarer" and

---

[19]Neruda's name for his house in the San Cristóbal hills overlooking the Santiago harbor and the right bank of the Mapocho River. The elaborate homage (*La chascona*) which concludes the *Memorial*, as a whole, however, synthesizes three of the poet's houses—Casa "La Chascona," Casa "La Sebastiana," in the Valparaíso hills, and his so-called "House in the Sand" at Isla Negra. For a picture book of Isla Negra, with photographs by Sergio Lorrain and a text in poetry and prose by Pablo Neruda, see *Una casa en la arena* (*A House in the Sand*) (Barcelona: Editorial Lumen, 1966).

"far-wanderer," and encircled by the ocean like a moat. How barbarously or how cunningly Neruda has built his vast *Memorial,* what artifacts, prophecies, legends and gods he has carried over his hearthstone, what enigmas still await him in island, mainland, and ocean, remain to be examined.

The critic's first task, confronted with the grandeurs and *longueurs* of this conception, must be a qualitative one: how to align the "memorial" with the "general," the "elemental," and the "ceremonial" as four phases in the orientation of a talent. I should like first of all to suggest that the "memorial" mode is *nonhistorical*: in Coleridge's words, it "emancipates [the poet] from the order of time and space,"[20] whereas the general, the elemental, and the ceremonial may be subsumed under it as modes and dimensions of the temporal. The dynamic that gave *Canto general* its unwearying sweep and thrust after three anguished *Residencias,* was history: history as the court chronicler and the anthropologist conceive it, and History as the polemical Marxist conceives it in an escalating dialectic of freedom and bondage. It is the historical mode, in this layman's understanding of the term, that induced Neruda to join his own chronicle with the perfidies and restorations of Chile, and the Creation story with a multinational saga of the death of kings, conquistadors, quislings, duces, and assorted "satraps" in a Century of Perishing Capital. His chronicle is roughly vertical in its sequences: into its rational progressions stream real wars, personal memoir, autobiography, topical villains and saviors, political reportage, global and national disasters, up to the final page, signed, in the poet's own hand, "today, 5 February, in this year / of 1949, in Chile, in 'Godomar / de Chena,' a few months before / the forty-fifth year of my life."

The pentad of Isla Negra, on the other hand, is concerned with memory rather than history. Into its five volumes there tumble a disorganized *recherche* of events, ruminations, obsessive image, words, doubts, allegiances, political man-

---

[20]S. T. Coleridge, *Biographia Literaria,* Chapter XIII.

dates and spiritual recoils in an *ordre du coeur* rather than
an *ordre raisonné.* Their point of departure and their point
of return are essentially the same: *time present,* in which the
poet, brooding daily on the change and the permanence of
things from a seacoast in Isla Negra, is induced to evoke an
answering dialectic from within. The dialectic is not Marx-
ian, but cosmological, and its polarizing genius is not History
but Memory—the same power invoked by St. Augustine as
"the belly of the mind"[21] in Book X of the *Confessions.* The
scene, for all its flashbacks into the displacements of a lifetime, is Isla Negra, to whose sea changes, cloudscapes, and
seasonal immediacies the poet constantly returns for a "residence on earth" fixed at last by the heart's choice and due
process of mortality.

Visitors to Isla Negra have, between jest and earnest, alluded
increasingly to the islanded Neruda as Buddha, guru, and
lama[22]—a kind of Latin amalgam of Merlin and Prospero.
More often than not, the epithets are irreverently, if affec-
tionately, intended: but the "saintly" Neruda, with his un-
flinching gaze on the "four perturbations of the mind:[23]
desire, joy, fear, sorrow"(*) and his Augustinian assault
upon Memory, is an exact distillation of the impact of the
Memorial. Coming into "the plains, caves, and caverns of
my memory"(*) from the secular engagements of a lifetime,
he says, almost in Augustine's words, "There meet I with

21*The Confessions of Saint Augustine,* edited, and with an introduction
by Arthur Symons (Walter Scott, Ltd.). All passages marked with an
asterisk are taken from this edition (undated) in the translation by
Pusey.

22Thus Selden Rodman, in "A Day with Pablo Neruda," *Saturday Review
of Literature,* July 9, 1966: "I saw him as a Buddha, ageless, perfectly
composed, with just the suggestion of a childlike smile around the
corners of his sensual mouth." And in a recent issue of *ABC* (Barcelona),
"Neruda como es," Luis María Anson writes: "The poet, converted into
a living god, an immutable Dalai Lama, reads an ode, heard with all
the intentness of a religious prayer."

23Cf. Neruda's *"las cuatro estaciones del alma"* (the four stations of the
soul), invoked in the concluding line of *"Cuanto pasa en un día"*:
"How Much Happens in a Day."

myself and recall myself, and when, where, and what I have done, and under what feelings."(∗):

> I also would see myself coming
> and know in the end how it feels to me
> when I come back to the place where I wait for myself
> and turn back to my sleep and die laughing.

The laughter of Neruda is a special dimension of the Hispanic—the Cervantine gift of the *quixotic,* in the presence of the Impossible, as it has flowed into the parlance of the world from the uplands of La Mancha. Like both Quixote and Augustine, however, Neruda is called back, out of History to the "reasons and laws innumerable of numbers and dimensions, none of which hath any bodily sense impressed,"(∗) and to the "deeper recesses" where "all must be drawn together again, that they may be known; that is to say, they must as it were be collected together from their dispersion"; and, indeed, "re-collected."(∗) Thus, we have Neruda's:

Memory

> All must be remembered:
> a turning wind, the threads
> in the threadbare event must be gathered,
> yard after yard of all we inhabited,
> the train's long trajectory,
> the trappings of sorrow.
>
> Should a rosebush be lost
> or the hare's track dissolve in the night,
> should the pillars of memory
> topple out of my reach,
> I must remake the air,
> the steam and the soil and the leaves . . .
>
> I was always an avid forgetter:
> in my two human hands
> only the untouchable things of the world
> live unscathed,

and the power of comparison
is the sum of their total destruction.

Forgetting, destroying, comparing, the human rememberer,
"toiling in the heavy soil"(∘) of his being, like Augustine,
discovers not sequence and consequence, but the plasm of
identity itself, the ego which has been the subject of the
poet's wonder in Whitman, in Hopkins, in Neruda, and
Aurelius Augustinus of Tagaste and Carthage. "What is
nearer to me than myself?" asks Augustine. "It is I myself
who remember, I the mind."(∘) Ransacking the world of
"things, either through images, as all bodies, or by actual
presence," he comes upon the mind's own testament of what
it has committed to memory, "that same memory where
before [all] lay unknown, scattered, and neglected."(∘)
Augustine has suggested the exaltation and despair of the
chase, with Nerudian avidity: "Over all these do I run, I
fly; I dive on this side and on that, as far I can, and there is
no end . . . Thus do I remember Carthage."(∘) And Eliot in
our own century has nodded acerb consent: "To apprehend
/ The point of intersection of the timeless / With time, is
an occupation for a saint."[24]

This I take to be both the task of Neruda's *Memorial,* and
a measure of its "sanctity" for which no fashionable mystique
need be sought. Again and again, over the record of personal
loves, circumstantial and topical particulars, names, dates,
habitations, concretions, a persisting query is heard, turning
the knowable into a "dangerous world"[25] of wandering lights
and haunted misgivings: "Who was I? What? What were we
both?" In a poem taking its title directly from Blake's great
archetype of spiritual quest, "Little Boy Lost," Neruda sug-
gests the malaise of the saintly identity:

> Nothing answers me now: let it pass.
> *Being* never was once: we went on being . . .
> All kept on happening,

---

[24]"The Dry Salvages," T. S. Eliot, *Four Quartets* (New York: Harcourt
Brace, 1943), p. 27.
[25]"Infant Sorrow," *Blake's Poetical Works,* edited by John Sampson
(London: Oxford University Press, 1938), p. 100.

one man impurely persisting,
son of the purely born son,
till nothing remained as it was . . .
Sometimes we remember
the presence that lived with us,
there is something we want from him—that he remember
    us, maybe,
or know, at least we were he and now talk
with his tongue,
but there in the wreckage of hours
he looks at us, acknowledging nothing.

The note is sounded again, plangent and ardent by turns, in "Those Lives":

"That's how I am," I'll say, leaving this
pretext in writing. "This is really my life."
But everyone knows that's not how it happens at all.
Not only the cords in the net, but the air
that escapes the interstices matters:
The rest remains as it was: inapprehensible.

and again:

I live as I can
in my destiny's ruthless lucidity,
between the luminous and the desperate halves,
disowned
by two kingdoms which never were mine.

and again:

Who is that Other I am? He who never
contrived how to smile and died of his perfect deprival?
Who outlasted the festival bells and the gala
carnation, and toppled the lecterns of cold?

Late, it grows late. I go on with it all. I pursue
this or that paradigm, never guessing the answer,

knowing myself, in each of the lives I have lived,
both absent and present, at once the man who I was,
  and I am.

Does the rub of mysterious verity lie there?

The quest for "mysterious verity" is constant throughout
these volumes of palpable and impalpable stock-taking, jar-
ring all that clings to the poet's ego, from its moorings in the
historical past. In the "memorial" world of Isla Negra, the
poet's *verdad* is exactly equivalent to the lover's search for
claridad in the *Sonnets*—with which it is eventually fused.
Keeping "steadfastly triangular," seeing all "at first hand,"
affirming the "power of the real to augment / and enlarge
us," yet "cherish[ing] the equivocal cut of my song," Neruda
writes "on the card of our hunger / an order of bread and
an order of soul for the table." For this purpose, he returns
to that most elusive and obsessive of his themes: the Song
of Myself, and its complementary theme of Non-Being—the
Ser-y-no-ser, the *Nada*, and the *Sueño* that link him to the
great Hispanic tradition of self-contemplation in Calderón,
in Unamuno, in Machado, in Guillén. It is in his unappeas-
able self-absorption, from *Twenty Love Poems and a Desperate Song*, up to the present—his solipsistic meditation on
the "water and rock" of "realism and idealism, both parts of
my world"—that his love and his desperation have their
source.

A closer look at the first of the five volumes of his *Memorial*
may help to illustrate. It begins, as did the concluding section of *Canto general* (flamboyantly entitled *Yo soy: I Am*)
twenty years before, with a retrospective account of the
childhood and the young manhood of the poet. The title of
the present volume, however, focuses upon a habitation
rather than a name, on a landscape rather than an ego:
Temuco of the alternate droughts and rains, the earthquakes, the timberlands, the holocausts—*Donde nace la
lluvia* (*Where the Rain Begins*). In his singularly appeal-

Ben Belitt / xxxix

ing essay on "Childhood and Poetry," published in 1954,[26] ten years before his *Memorial*, Neruda has given us a prose recitative for his Song of Temuco: a personal history from the days of his great-great-grandparents who planted their vines in Parral, to the remarriage of his father, "a nondescript farmer, a mediocre laborer, but a first-class railroader," and his removal to Temuco.

It would appear that Neruda has deliberately set out, in *Where the Rain Begins*, to produce a versified "Childhood and Poetry"—a kind of Wordsworthian *Prelude* to a chronicle of wanderings and revolution, over which the "Spirit of the Place" broods to the end, as the Lake Country broods over the musings of Wordsworth. Where the prose chronicler informs us, for example, that "My mother could pick out in the dark, among all the other trains, precisely the train that was bringing my father into the Stationhouse at Temuco or taking him away," the Spirit of the Place remembers: "The brusque father comes back / from his trains: / we could pick out / his train whistle / cutting the rain, a locomotive's / nocturnal lament / in the dark. Later / the door started trembling." The plank houses, alternately soaking and burning, the mother "dead in Parral not long after I was born," the "tutelary angel" of his father's remarriage, Doña Trinidad Candia, the "glacial" cold of the Temucan schoolhouse, the midsummer forays into the Araucanian forests, the "searing" Cautín and the summits of Nielal, the swans of Lake Budi, the green plums, the beetles, the *copihues*, the secret world of Sandokan and Sandokana,[27] and above all, the omnipresent whistle of the night train cutting fatefully through flood, distances, and darkness with the wail of a vanished paternity—all are transcribed from the essayist's pages.

Here, it would appear, History and Memory are well

---

[26]Reprinted in the *Obras completas*, 1957, pp. 19–30. Translated, with certain omissions, by Ben Belitt, under the title "A Pine Cone, A Toy Sheep. . . ." in *Evergreen Review*, Vol. 6, No. 22, Jan.–Feb. 1962, pp. 22–35. Reprinted in *Evergreen Review Reader* (New York: Grove Press, 1968).

[27]Hero and heroine of the piratical *Sandokan* by Emilio Salgari (1863–1911), nostalgically invoked by Neruda in his "Childhood and Poetry."

matched. The way is vertical, if circuitous, and the elements are in sequence: Birth, First Journey, The Stepmother (*La Mamadre*), The Father, The First Ocean, The Southern Earth, Winter School, Sex, Poetry, Timidity, Swan Lake—such, literally, is the order of his book. Precisely when all is in readiness for a triumphal affirmation of consciousness, however, the Spirit of the Place materializes like a wraith to protest the poet's total disbelief in the buoyant historicity of his chronicle. The pivot which triggers his melancholy significantly takes its title from the poem by Blake already referred to: "Little Boy Lost" (*"El niño perdido"*) and the theme of loss—*"lo perdido"*—is thereafter never absent from the long circuit of the *Memorial*. As it happens, the word is one of the most multiple—and therefore least translatable—in the rich overlay of its contexts in Spanish. Beginning somewhat lamely with its nominal denotation—"lost"—it traverses an equivocal spectrum from "vanished," "absent," "lapsed," "destroyed," "forgotten," "fallen," to "dead"—always with a nostalgic look backward. Its blood cousin, the multifaceted word to which it generally points, like a needle to a magnet, is *soledad,* or aloneness, loneliness, isolation, self-engrossment, intactness, alienation. Between, whirls a mob of grieving mutations: *confuso* (confused), *secreto* (secret), *indeciso* (indecisive), *enlutado* (mournful)—the *no-sé-qué* (I-don't-know-what) of empirical metaphysics on its way to the limbo of the *No-Ser* (Non-Being).

A sampling of the pages of *Where the Rain Begins* must suffice to suggest both the persistence of the lost (*lo perdido*) and its absorption into the spectrum of the solitary (*soledad*). There are *pasos perdidos* (lost footsteps), *fiebre o alas perdidas* (lost fever or wings), *bodega perdida entre las trenes* (shop lost among trains), *grité perdido* (I cried out, lost), *se perdía mi infancia* (my childhood was lost), *perdí los arboles* (I lost the trees), and the *estudiante triste perdido en el crepúsculo* (sad schoolboy lost in the twilight) —which brings the poet up to the publication of his second volume, *Crepusculario, The Book of Twilight*. In between, glows an *ignis fatuus* of flickering modulations which are the special illumination of the memory asserting its bafflement at the intersection of time with the timeless. Here, too, the contexts are diverse: *se me confundo los ojos y las hojas* (my eyes and the leaves are confused), *la confusa soledad* (the confused solitude), *una luz indecisa* (an indecisive light), *entro indeciso* (I enter undecided), *la enlutada noche* (the mournful night), *yo, enlutado, severo, ausente* (I, mournful, severe, absent), *volví con el secreto* (I returned with the secret), *en el secreto mundo / caminamos / con respeto* (in the secret world / we walk / with respect), *no distingo entre labios y raíces* (I do not distinguish between lips and roots), *no sé, no sé de donde* (I don't know, I don't know whence), *no sabía qué decir, mi boca / no sabía / nombrar* (I did not know what to say, my mouth did not know how to name).

Specification is in order here because the total effect, in *Black Island Memorial*, flickers from point to point like marsh gas, with no expectation of an explosive outcome. It is not given to Neruda, as agonist of the Lost, to cover his eyes in the presence of the mind's transfiguration: neither blinded nor prostrate, he looks steadily into the impurities of duration—animal, vegetal, and mineral,

> while a luster is borne underground, antiquity's
>   princeling
> in his natural grave-clothes of sickening mineral,
> until we are tardily there, too late to be there at all:
> being and not being, life takes its being from these.

Only once is he permitted to see "plainly: one evening, / in India" when, gazing steadily into the flames of a riverside suttee, he sees "something move out of the burning sarcophagus / —call it smoke or a spirit—" and remains until all is consumed, leaving only "night and the water, the dark / and the river, steadfast in that place and that dying." The world's body and the combustion of the world's body: these are the themes of the saint's vigil and man's image of the world's loss.

The point finally to be made, in this uneasy reading of an equivocal legend, is that the *perdido* pursues Neruda throughout the whole compass of his *Memorial,* as a function, rather than a defection, of memory. One could, I am sure, make a tidy case for the first four volumes as the poet's odyssey or hegira through all four elements of the substantive universe—(1) Water (*Donde nace la lluvia: Where the Rain Begins*), (2) Air (*La luna en el laberinto: The Moon in the Labyrinth*), (3) Fire (*El cruel fuego: The Cruel Fire*), and (4) Earth (*El cazador de raices: The Root-Hunter*). Since History and Memory weave themselves equally into his great design, it might be specified for the curious that Water is cognate with the poet's Temucan childhood, Air, with the erotic and the passional, Fire, with revolutionary upheaval and world war, and Earth with the poet's return to his sources on the Chilean mainland: a thoroughly Blakean cosmology. Over this tidy collocation of elements and events, however, as over the burning suttee, moves the Spirit of the Place, surrounded by all the paraphernalia of quantitative optimism,[28] brooding on the Lost. If there is any question regarding the persistence of the Lost, one has only to follow the path of the *perdido* into the fifth and final volume, which Neruda somewhat misleadingly has entitled *Sonata crítica* (*Critical Sonata*), as though disengagement and perspective had at last been achieved. Here the tally is no less obliterating than in Book One: Neruda, as card player, "plays for the sake of losing" (*juego / para seguir perdiendo*); he is "lost in the night" (*perdido en la noche*); "there is no longer left [him] a place to lose / the key, the truth, or the lie" (*no hay donde perder / la llave, la verdad, ni la mentira*); we have "all lost the battle" (*todos perdimos la batalla*); "the truth has died" (*ya se murió la verdad*); humanity "loses its way" (*esta humanidad que pierde el rumbo*); the pure being is "lost between words" (*el casto ser perdido entre palabras*); life is "passed or lost" (*cuanta vida / pasamos o perdimos*); memory "trembles in the lost shadow" (*tiembla mi memoria en la sombra perdida*); the "salt is scattered and lost" (*una sal esparcida y perdida*); the wind's sigh remains "lost in the leaves" (*sigue el susurro del viento perdido en las*

---

[28]Recall the iconography of Dürer's "Melancholia."

hojas); but, none the less, "I have found my lost roots" (*encontré mis raices perdidos*).

It would be both mischievous and myopic to suggest on the basis of such passages that *Black Island Memorial* is the labyrinthine complaint of a defeated and despairing man. On the contrary, Neruda's steadfast confrontation of the Lost, his avid immediacies and open-ended determination to live "between the luminous and the desperate halves," measure the strenuous vitalism of his position. It is the Muse of Memory, as Keats' *Hyperion* was also to discover in the fallen world of Titans, sifting the passing event for its "Names, deeds, gray legends, dire events, rebellions, / Majesties, sovran voices, agonies, / Creations and destroyings"[29] that "shows the heart's secret to an ancient power" with an intimacy impossible to History. And it is the double vision of the later Neruda, committed equally to Mnemosyne and Clio, that demands an exact accounting from the poet of "what is past, and passing, and to come."[30] Neruda, looking back at his bulking *Memorial*, unfinished to the very end, declares in the *Critical Sonata*: "He who sings both dies and does not die, he who sings goes on living and dying"; he "sings the earthly and heavenly tower from the abyss." It is thus that the *poeta enlutado,* reading the oceans and weathers of Black Island, construing interstices, gaps, collapses, losses, with a passion that dazzles the imagination, holds in his keeping the plenty and certainty of the world. No poet living has braced the whole of his talent on that "point of intersection of the timeless / With time" with a comparable freedom from cant and preconception, or more resolutely approximated the "occupation for a saint."

Some matters require grateful acknowledgment at this time. The collaboration of Alastair Reid is a kindness for which both the poet and myself have reason to be especially thank-

---

[29]"Hyperion," *The Poetical Works of John Keats,* edited by H. W. Garrod (New York, London, Toronto: Oxford University Press, 1956), p. 242.

[30]"Sailing to Byzantium," *The Collected Poems of W. B. Yeats* (New York: Macmillan, 1951), p. 192.

ful, and should speak for our joint conviction of the pluralism of the translator's art, the multiplicity of Pablo Neruda, and the possibility, as Mr. Reid has put it, that "just as there is no single correct translation, there may in fact be no single definitive original." My thanks are also due to the National Institute of Arts and Letters and the National Endowment for the Arts for a sabbatical grant which has allowed me to work uninterruptedly at a task that might otherwise have required months or years of gerrymandered time; to Bennington College, for both a leave of absence and the Fels Faculty Fund that sponsored a final draft of this manuscript; to certain periodicals that published the Introduction in essay form: *The Southern Review*, *Mundus Artium*, *Voyages*, and in Spanish translations by Ulises Picco in *Mundo Nuevo* (Paris) and *Razón y Fábula* (Bogotá); and to various publications in which certain of these translations have previously appeared: *The New York Times Book Review*, *The Bennington Review*, *Evergreen Review*, *Poetry*, *The Nation*, *The Southern Review*, *Mundus Artium*, *Tri-Quarterly*, *Encounter* (London), and *Voyages*.

I should like finally to acknowledge a bond which, but for a series of postal misadventures, might well have turned into a debt, to E. Rodríguez Monegal, whose sensitive and scrupulous study of Neruda, *The Immobile Traveler*,[31] reached me too late for inclusion in this preface. With the publication of this volume, there is no longer any need to deplore either the monotony or the insularity of South American criticism, or to doubt that it is in the best possible hands. Curiously enough, it has remained for a fellow-countryman of de Lautréamont and Laforgue to mediate among the many worlds of Pablo Neruda, as though the heights of Macchu Picchu required the middle distance of Montevideo to preside over a poet's perspective of spiritual change, and open windows toward Europe. Our identity of concern in certain matters, including the motif of the "little boy lost" and the dynamics of Memory, not only persuades

---

[31]*El viajero inmóvil: introducción a Pablo Neruda* (Buenos Aires: Editorial Losada, 1966).

me of the rightness of many lonely choices, but of time's fullness, which has already absorbed Neruda into that kinship which makes all literatures and all ideas of excellence one.

Bennington College
Bennington, Vermont

Estravagario / Book of Vagaries
1958

humerous, ironic book
marks the beginning of his
autumnal stage

— deconstruction of his formal selves
not typical of Neruda

central theme - identity

Translated by Alastair Reid

POBRES MUCHACHOS

Cómo cuesta en este planeta
amarnos con tranquilidad:
todo el mundo mira las sábanas,
todos molestan a tu amor.

Y se cuentan cosas terribles
de un hombre y de una mujer
que después de muchos trajines
y muchas consideraciones
hacen algo insustituíble,
se acuestan en una sola cama.

Yo me pregunto si las ranas
se vigilan y se estornudan,
si se susurran en las charcas
contra las ranas ilegales,
contra el placer de los batracios.
Yo me pregunto si los pájaros
tienen pájaros enemigos
y si el toro escucha a los bueyes
antes de verse con la vaca.

Ya los caminos tienen ojos,
los parques tienen policía,
son sigilosos los hoteles,
las ventanas anotan nombres,
se embarcan tropas y cañones
decididos contra el amor,
trabajan incesantemente
las gargantas y las orejas,
y un muchacho con su muchacha
se obligaron a florecer
volando en una bicicleta.

POOR FELLOWS

What it costs us, on this planet,
to make love to each other in peace.
The whole world has its eye on the sheets.
They all trouble your loving.

And they tell fearful tales
involving a man and a woman
who, after many wanderings,
and with proper consideration,
achieve something unique—
they lie together in one bed.

I wonder to myself if frogs
spy on each other and sneeze,
if they are muttering in the frog pools
against delinquent frogs,
against the pleasures of amphibians.
I wonder to myself if the birds
have it in for other birds,
if the bull eavesdrops on the oxen
before going with his cow.

Even the roads have eyes.
The parks include policemen.
The hotels are furtive.
The windows take down names.
Troops and cannon embark,
mobilized against loving.
Both ears and voices
are ceaselessly at work,
and any fellow with his girl
has been obliged to find pleasure
in flight on a bicycle.

Pablo Neruda / 3

CABALLOS

Ví desde la ventana los caballos.

Fué en Berlín, en invierno. La luz
era sin luz, sin cielo el cielo.

El aire blanco como un pan mojado.

Y desde mi ventana un solitario circo
mordido por los dientes del invierno.

De pronto, conducidos por un hombre,
diez caballos salieron a la niebla.

Apenas ondularon al salir, como el fuego,
pero para mis ojos ocuparon el mundo
vacío hasta esa hora. Perfectos, encendidos,
eran como diez dioses de largas patas puras,
de crines parecidas al sueño de la sal.

Sus grupas eran mundos y naranjas.

Su color era miel, ámbar, incendio.

Sus cuellos eran torres
cortadas en la piedra del orgullo,
y a los ojos furiosos se asomaba
como una prisionera, la energía.

Y allí en silencio, en medio
del día, del invierno sucio y desordenado,
los caballos intensos eran la sangre,
el ritmo, el incitante tesoro de la vida.

Miré, miré y entonces reviví: sin saberlo
allí estaba la fuente, la danza de oro, el cielo,
el fuego que vivía en la belleza.

He olvidado el invierno de aquel Berlín oscuro.

No olvidaré la luz de los caballos.

HORSES

It was from the window I saw the horses.

I was in Berlin, in winter. The light
was without light, the sky skyless.

The air white like a moistened loaf.

From my window, I could see a deserted arena,
a circle bitten out by the teeth of winter.

All at once, led out by a man,
ten horses were stepping into the snow.

Emerging, they had scarcely rippled into existence
like flame, than they filled the whole world of my eyes,
empty till now. Faultless, flaming,
they stepped like ten gods on broad, clean hooves,
their manes recalling a dream of pure grace.

Their rumps were globes, were oranges.

Their color was amber and honey, was on fire.

Their necks were towers
carved from the stone of pride,
and in their furious eyes, sheer energy
showed itself, a prisoner inside them.

And there, in the silence, at the mid-
point of the day, in a dirty, disgruntled winter,
the horses' intense presence was blood,
was rhythm, was the beckoning Grail of being.

I saw, I saw, and, seeing, I came to life.
There was the unwitting fountain, the dance of gold, the sky,
the fire that sprang to life in beautiful things.

I have obliterated that gloomy Berlin winter.

I shall not forget the light from these horses.

Pablo Neruda / 5

CUANTO PASA EN UN DÍA

Dentro de un día nos veremos.

Pero en un día crecen cosas,
se venden uvas en la calle,
cambia la piel de los tomates,
la muchacha que te gustaba
no volvió más a la oficina.

Cambiaron de pronto el cartero.
Las cartas ya no son las mismas.
Varias hojas de oro y es otro:
este árbol es ahora un rico.

Quién nos diría que la tierra
con su vieja piel cambia tanto?
Tiene más volcanes que ayer,
el cielo tiene nuevas nubes,
los ríos van de otra manera.
Además cuánto se construye! *→ el humano cambia al mundo*
Yo he inaugurado centenares
de carreteras, de edificios,
de puentes puros y delgados
como navíos o violines.

Por eso cuando te saludo
y beso tu boca florida
nuestros besos son otros besos
y nuestras bocas otras bocas.

Salud, amor, salud por todo
lo que cae y lo que florece.

Salud por ayer y por hoy,
por anteayer y por mañana.

Salud por el pan y la piedra,
salud por el fuego y la lluvia.

HOW MUCH HAPPENS IN A DAY

In the course of a day, we shall meet one another.

But, in one day, things spring up—
they sell grapes in the street,
tomatoes change their skin,
the young girl you fancied
did not come back to the office.

They changed the postman suddenly.
The letters now are not the same.
A few golden leaves and it's changed;
this tree is now rich.

Who would have said that the earth
with its ancient skin would change so much?
It has more volcanoes than yesterday,
the sky has new clouds,
the rivers are flowing differently.
Besides, so much has come into being!
I have inaugurated hundreds
of highways and buildings,
delicate, clean bridges
like ships or violins.

And so, when I greet you
and kiss your flowering mouth,
our kisses are other kisses,
our mouths are new mouths.

Joy, my love, joy in all things,
what falls and what flourishes.

Joy in today and yesterday,
the day before and tomorrow.

Joy in bread and stone,
in fire and in rain.

Pablo Neruda / 7

Por lo que cambia, nace, crece,
se consume y vuelve a ser beso.

[handwritten: — la vida es un culo]

Salud por lo que tenemos de aire
y lo que tenemos de tierra.

Cuando se seca nuestra vida
nos quedan sólo las raíces
y el viento es frío como el odio.

[handwritten: → cuando se acaba la vida]

Entonces cambiamos de piel,
de uñas, de sangre, de mirada,
y tú me besas y yo salgo
a vender luz por los caminos.

Salud por la noche y el día
y las cuatro estaciones del alma.

[handwritten: niñez, adolescencia, adulto, anciano]

In what changes, is born, grows,
consumes itself, and becomes a kiss again.

Joy in the air we have,
and in what we have of earth.

When our life has dried up,
only the roots remain to us,
and the wind is cold like hate.

Then let us change our skin,
our nails, our blood, our gazing;
you kiss me and I go out
to sell light on the roads.

Joy in the night and the day,
and the four stations of the soul.

Pablo Neruda / 9

Cuál es el cuál, cuál es el cómo?
Quién sabe cómo conducirse?

Qué naturales son los peces!
Nunca parecen inoportunos.
Están en el mar invitados
y se visten correctamente
sin una escama de menos,
condecorados por el agua.

Yo todos los días pongo
no sólo los pies en el plato,
sino los codos, los riñones,
la lira, el alma, la escopeta.

No sé qué hacer con las manos
pero dónde pongo el anillo?
y he pensado venir sin ellas,
Qué pavorosa incertidumbre!

Y luego no conozco a nadie.
No recuerdo sus apellidos.

—Me parece conocer a Ud.
—No es Ud. un contrabandista?
—Y Ud. señora no es la amante
del alcohólico poeta
que se paseaba sin cesar,
sin rumbo fijo por las cornisas?
—Voló porque tenía alas.
—Y Ud. continúa terrestre.
—Me gustaría haberla entregado
como india viuda a un gran brasero,
no podríamos quemarla ahora?
Resultaría palpitante!

APROPOS MY BAD EDUCATION

Which is which, which is how:
Who knows how to conduct himself?

How natural the fish seem!
They never seem out of order.
In the sea, they are guests,
and always dress correctly,
never a scale too few,
bemedaled by the water.

But I—every day I put
not only my feet on the plate
but my elbows too, and my kidneys,
lyre, soul and shotgun.

I don't know what to do with my hands,
and have thought of coming without them,
but where do I put my ring?
What feeble uncertainty!

*ironic: the not knowing why some-
thing is needed, but knowing
you need it.*

And ultimately, I know no one.
I do not remember their names.

You seem familiar to me.
Are you not a smuggler?
And you, Madam, aren't you the lover
of the alcoholic poet
who walked and walked endlessly,
aimlessly over the rooftops?
He flew because he had wings.
And you continue earthbound.
I should like to have delivered her
like an Indian widow to a great furnace.
Could we not burn her now?
It would be breathtaking!

Otra vez en una Embajada
me enamoré de una morena,
no quiso desnudarse allí,
y yo se lo increpé con dureza:
estás loca, estatua silvestre,
cómo puedes andar vestida?

Me desterraron duramente
de esa y de otras reuniones,
si por error me aproximaba
cerraban ventanas y puertas.

Anduve entonces con gitanos
y con prestidigitadores,
con marineros sin buque,
con pescadores sin pescado,
pero todos tenían reglas,
inconcebibles protocolos
y mi educación lamentable
me trajo malas consecuencias.

Por eso no voy y no vengo,
no me visto ni ando desnudo,
eché al pozo los tenedores,
las cucharas y los cuchillos.
Sólo me sonrío a mí solo,
no hago preguntas indiscretas
y cuando vienen a buscarme,
con gran honor, a los banquetes,
mando mi ropa, mis zapatos,
mi camisa con mi sombrero,
pero aún así no se contentan:
iba sin corbata mi traje.

Así para salir de dudas
me decidí a una vida honrada
de la más activa pereza,
purifiqué mis intenciones,
salí a comer conmigo solo

Another time, in an Embassy,
I fell in love with a brunette.
She would not undress there
and I rebuked her stiffly—
you are mad, my wild statue,
how can you move in your clothes?

They banished me brutally
from that and from other gatherings,
and if by mistake I approached,
they closed windows and doors.

I went then with gypsies
and with magicians,
shipless seafarers,
fishermen with no fish,
but all of them had their rules,
unbelievable protocols,
and my wretched education
brought me bad consequences.

So I neither go nor come,
neither dress nor walk naked.
In the well, I dropped the forks,
the spoons and the knives.
I smile at myself alone,
never ask indiscreet questions,
and when they come to bring me
to banquets, with great pomp,
I send my clothes—my shoes,
my shirt and my hat,
but even that does not please them—
my jacket was without a tie.

So, to be free of doubts,
I settled for an honorable life,
as actively lazy as possible.
I purified my intentions,
went out to dine alone with myself,

y así me fuí quedando mudo.
A veces me saqué a bailar,
pero sin gran entusiasmo,
y me acuesto solo, sin ganas,
por no equivocarme de cuarto.

Adiós, porque vengo llegando.

Buenos días, me voy de prisa.

Cuando quieran verme ya saben:
búsquenme donde no estoy
y si les sobra tiempo y boca
pueden hablar con mi retrato.

And so I left, keeping my silence.
Sometimes I dragged myself off to a dance
but without much enthusiasm,
and I bedded alone, not wanting to,
so as not to mistake my room.

Goodbye, because here I am arriving.

Good morning, I'm off in a hurry.

When they wish to see me, now they know.
Let them look for me where I am not,
and if they have voice and time left,
they may converse with my portrait.

AL PIE DESDE SU NIÑO

El pie del niño aún no sabe que es pie,
y quiere ser mariposa o manzana.

Pero luego los vidrios y las piedras,
las calles, las escaleras,
y los caminos de la tierra dura
van enseñando al pie que no puede volar,
que no puede ser fruto redondo en una rama.
El pie del niño entonces
fué derrotado, cayó
en la batalla,
fué prisionero,
condenado a vivir en un zapato.

Poco a poco sin luz
fué conociendo el mundo a su manera,
sin conocer el otro pie, encerrado
explorando la vida como un ciego.

Aquellas suaves uñas
de cuarzo, de racimo,
se endurecieron, se mudaron
en opaca substancia, en cuerno duro,
y los pequeños pétalos del niño
se aplastaron, se desequilibraron,
tomaron formas de reptil sin ojos,
cabezas triangulares de gusano.
Y luego encallecieron,
se cubrieron
con mínimos volcanes de la muerte,
inaceptables endurecimientos.

Pero este ciego anduvo
sin tregua, sin parar
hora tras hora,
el pie y el otro pie,
ahora de hombre

TO THE FOOT FROM ITS CHILD

The child's foot is not yet aware it's a foot,
and wants to be a butterfly or an apple.

But later, stones and glass shards,
streets, ladders,
and the paths in the rough earth
go on teaching the foot it cannot fly,
cannot be a fruit swollen on the branch.
Then, the child's foot
was defeated, fell
in the battle,
was a prisoner
condemned to live in a shoe.

Bit by bit, in that dark,
it grew to know the world in its own way,
out of touch with its fellow, enclosed,
feeling out life like a blind man.

These soft nails
of quartz, bunched together,
grew hard, and changed themselves
into opaque substance, hard as horn,
and the tiny, petaled toes of the child
grew bunched and out of trim,
took on the form of eyeless reptiles
with triangular heads, like worms.
Later, they grew calloused
and were covered
with the faint volcanoes of death,
a coarsening hard to accept.

But this blind thing walked
without respite, never stopping
for hour after hour,
the one foot, the other,
now the man's,

o de mujer,
arriba,
abajo,
por los campos, las minas,
los almacenes y los ministerios,
atrás,
afuera, adentro,
adelante,
este pie trabajó con su zapato,
apenas tuvo tiempo
de estar desnudo en el amor o el sueño,
caminó, caminaron
hasta que el hombre entero se detuvo.

Y entonces a la tierra
bajó y no supo nada,
porque allí todo y todo estaba oscuro,
no supo que había dejado de ser pie
si lo enterraban para que volara
o para que pudiera
ser manzana.

now the woman's,
up above,
down below,
through fields, mines,
markets and ministries,
backward,
far afield, inward,
forward,
this foot toiled in its shoe,
scarcely taking time
to bare itself in love or sleep;
it walked, they walked,
until the whole man chose to stop.

And then it descended
to earth, and knew nothing,
for there, everything everywhere was dark.
It did not know it had ceased to be a foot,
or if they were burying it so that it might fly,
or so that it might become
an apple.

SUEÑOS DE TRENES

Estaban soñando los trenes
en la estación, indefensos,
sin locomotoras, dormidos.

Entré titubeando en la aurora: —> madrugada
anduve buscando secretos,
cosas perdidas en los vagones,
en el olor muerto del viaje.
Entre los cuerpos que partieron
me senté solo en el tren inmóvil.

Era compacto el aire, un bloque
de conversaciones caídas
y fugitivos desalientos.
Almas perdidas en los trenes
como llaves sin cerraduras
caídas bajo los asientos.

Pasajeras del Sur cargadas
de ramilletes y gallinas,
tal vez fueron asesinadas,
tal vez volvieron y lloraron,
tal vez gastaron los vagones
con el fuego de sus claveles:
tal vez yo viajo, estoy con ellas,
tal vez el vapor de los viajes,
los rieles mojados, tal vez
todo vive en el tren inmóvil
y yo un pasajero dormido
desdichadamente despierto.

Yo estuve sentado y el tren
andaba dentro de mi cuerpo,
aniquilando mis fronteras,
de pronto era el tren de la infancia,
el humo de la madrugada,
el verano alegre y amargo.

A DREAM OF TRAINS

The trains were dreaming in
the station, defenseless,
engineless, asleep.

I entered uncertainly at dawn.
I went looking for secrets,
things left behind in the wagons,
in the leftover smell of the journey.
Among departing souls, I felt
myself alone in the motionless train.

The air was thick, a block
of compressed conversations
and passing depressions—
lost souls in the corridors
like keys without locks
fallen under the seats.

Women traveling from the South, laden
with bunches of flowers and chickens;
perhaps they were murdered,
perhaps they returned and wept,
perhaps they consumed the carriages
with their carnations' fire,
perhaps I am traveling, along with them,
perhaps the steam of the journey,
the wet rails, perhaps
all of them live in the stationary train,
and I am a sleeping passenger
waking up suddenly in misery.

I was in my seat and the train
was running through my body,
breaking down my frontiers—
suddenly, it was the train of my childhood,
smoke of the early morning,
bittersweetness of summer.

Eran otros trenes que huían,
carros repletos de dolores,
cargados como con asfalto,
y así corría el tren inmóvil
en la mañana que crecía
dolorosa sobre mis huesos.

Yo estaba solo en el tren solo,
pero no sólo estaba solo,
sino que muchas soledades
allí se habrán congregado
esperando para viajar
como pobres en los andenes.
Y yo en el tren como humo muerto
con tantos inasibles seres,
por tantas muertes agobiado
me sentí perdido en un viaje
en el que nada se movía,
sino mi corazón cansado.

There were other trains which fled,
their cars well-filled with sorrows,
like a cargo of asphalt;
so did the stationary train run on
in the morning which was growing
heavy about my bones.

I was alone in the solitary train,
but not only was I alone—
a host of solitudes were gathered
in the hope of the journey,
like peasants on the platforms.
And I, in the train, like stale smoke,
with so many shiftless souls,
burdened by so many deaths,
felt myself lost on a journey
in which nothing was moving
save my exhausted heart.

PARTENOGÉNESIS

Todos los que me daban consejos
están más locos cada día.
Por suerte no les hice caso
y se fueron a otra ciudad
en donde viven todos juntos
intercambiándose sombreros.

Eran sujetos estimables,
políticamente profundos,
y cada falta que yo hacía
les causaba tal sufrimiento
que encanecieron, se arrugaron,
dejaron de comer castañas, *chestnuts*
y una otoñal melancolía
por fin los dejó delirantes.

quote in essay

Ahora yo no sé qué ser,
si olvidadizo o respetuoso,
si continuar aconsejado
o reprocharles su delirio:
no sirvo para independiente,
me pierdo entre tanto follaje,
y no sé si salir o entrar,
si caminar o detenerme,
si comprar gatos o tomates.

Voy a tratar de comprender
lo que no debo hacer y hacerlo,
y así poder justificar
los caminos que se me pierdan,
porque si yo no me equivoco
quién va a creer en mis errores?
Si continúo siendo sabio
nadie me va a tomar en cuenta.

Pero trataré de cambiar:
voy a saludar con esmero,

PARTHENOGENESIS

All those who would give me advice
seem even madder every day.
Luckily they did not mind
and went to another city
where the people all live together
constantly swapping sombreros.

They were worthy subjects,
politically thoughtful,
and every fault I perpetrated
caused them such suffering
that they turned gray and wrinkled,
gave up eating chestnuts,
and an autumnal melancholy
finally left them delirious.

Now I do not know what to be—
forgetful or respectful;
to continue to give them counsel
or reproach them for their madness.
I cannot claim independence.
I am lost in so much foliage,
not knowing whether to leave or enter,
to travel or to linger,
to buy cats or tomatoes.

I shall try to understand
what I must not do, then do it
so to be able to justify
where I go astray,
for if I do not make mistakes,
who will believe that I err?
If I go on being wise,
no one will notice me.

But I shall try to change,
offer greetings with great care

voy a cuidar las apariencias
con dedicación y entusiasmo
hasta ser todo lo que quieran
que uno sea y que uno no sea,
hasta no ser sino los otros.

Y entonces si me dejan tranquilo
me voy a cambiar de persona,
voy a discrepar de pellejo,
y cuando ya tenga otra boca,
otros zapatos, otros ojos,
cuando ya sea diferente
y nadie pueda conocerme
seguiré haciendo lo mismo
porque no sé hacer otra cosa.

and look to appearances
with dedication and zeal
until I am all that they wish,
as one might be and another might not,
till I am not, except in others.

And then, if they leave me in peace,
I am going to change my nature,
and differ with my skin;
and when I have another mouth,
other shoes, other eyes;
when it is then all changed,
and no one can recognize me,
since anything else is beyond me,
I shall go on doing the same.

theme of different selves

rebirth

REGRESO A UNA CIUDAD

A qué he venido? les pregunto.

Quién soy en esta ciudad muerta?

No encuentro la calle ni el techo
de la loca que me quería.

Los cuervos, no hay duda, en las ramas,
mi rostro recién resurrecto.
el Monzón verde y furibundo,
el escupitajo escarlata
en las calles desmoronadas,
el aire espeso, pero dónde,
pero dónde estuve, quién fuí?
No entiendo sino las cenizas.

El vendedor de betel mira
sin reconocer mis zapatos,
Tal vez su abuelo me diría:
"Salam" pero sucede
que se cayó mientras volaba,
se cayó al pozo de la muerte.

En tal edificio dormí
catorce meses y sus años,
escribí desdichas,
mordí
la inocencia de la amargura,
y ahora paso y no está la puerta:
la lluvia ha trabajado mucho.

Ahora me doy cuenta que he sido
no sólo un hombre sino varios
y que cuantas veces he muerto,
sin saber cómo he revivido,
como si cambiara de traje
me puse a vivir otra vida

RETURN TO A CITY

What have I arrived in? I ask them.

Who am I in this lifeless city?

I can find neither the street nor the roof
of the crazy girl who once loved me.

There's no doubting the crows in the branches,
The monsoon green and boiling,
the scarlet spittle
in the eroded streets,
the air heavy—but where,
where was I, who was I?
I understand little, except the ashes.

The betel-seller looks at me,
recognizing neither my shoes
nor my recently resurrected face.
Perhaps his grandmother would grant me
a salaam, but it so happens
that she succumbed while I was traveling,
dropped deep into the well of death.

I slept in such a building
fourteen months and the corresponding years;
I wrote out my misery.
I bit
innocently into bitterness.
I pass now and the door is not there.
The rain has been working overtime.

Now it dawns on me that I have been
not just one man but several,
and that I have died so many times
with no notion of how I was reborn,
as if the act of changing clothes
were to force me to live another life,

y aquí me tienen sin que sepa
por qué no reconozco a nadie,
por qué nadie me reconoce,
si todos fallecieron aquí
y yo soy entre tanto olvido
un pájaro sobreviviente
o al revés la ciudad me mira
y sabe que yo soy un muerto.

Ando por bazares de seda
y por mercados miserables,
me cuesta creer que las calles
son las mismas, los ojos negros
duros como puntas de clavo
golpean contra mis miradas,
y la pálida Pagoda de Oro
con su inmóvil idolatría
ya no tiene ojos, ya no tiene
manos, ya no tiene fuego.
Adiós, calles sucias del tiempo,
adiós, adiós amor perdido,
regreso al vino de mi casa,
regreso al amor de mi amada,
a lo que fuí y a lo que soy,
agua y sol, tierras con manzanas,
meses con labios y con nombres,
regreso para no volver,
nunca más quiero equivocarme,
es peligroso caminar
hacia atrás porque de repente
es una cárcel el pasado.

and here I am without the least idea
of why I cannot recognize a soul,
of why no one is recognizing me,
as if everyone here were dead
and I alive in the midst of such forgetting,
a bird that still survives—
or, the reverse, the city watches me,
and realizes I am the one who is dead.

I walk through the silk bazaars,
and the markets of wretchedness.
It is hard to believe in the streets
as the selfsame streets, in the black eyes,
hard as nailpoints,
which glare back against my glances,
and in the pale Golden Pagoda
with all its frozen idolatry;
it has no eyes now, no hands,
no longer any fire.
Goodbye, streets soiled by time,
goodbye, goodbye, lost love.
I return to the wine of my house,
I return to the love of my loved one,
to what I was and to what I am,
water and sun, earth ripe with apples,
months with lips and with names.
I return not to come back;
no more do I wish to mislead myself.
It is dangerous to wander
backward, for all of a sudden
it is a prison, the past.

Ay qué Sábados más profundos!

Es interesante el planeta
con tanta gente en movimiento:
olas de pies en los hoteles,
urgentes motociclistas,
ferrocarriles hacia el mar
y cuántas muchachas inmóviles
raptadas por rápidas ruedas.

Todas las Semanas terminan
en hombres, mujeres y arena,
y hay que correr, no perder nada,
vencer inútiles colinas,
masticar música insoluble,
volver cansados al cemento.

Yo bebo por todos los Sábados
sin olvidar al prisionero
detrás de las paredes crueles:
ya no tienen nombre sus días
y este rumor que cruza y corre
lo rodea como el océano
sin conocer cuál es la ola,
la ola del húmedo Sábado.

Ay qué Sábados irritantes
armados de bocas y piernas,
desenfrenadas, de carrera,
bebiendo más de lo prudente:
no protestemos del bullicio
que no quiere andar con nosotros.

OH, WHAT BOTTOMLESS SATURDAYS!

Oh, what bottomless Saturdays!

Fascinating, this planet,
with so many people in motion:
waves of feet in the hotels,
impatient motorcyclists,
railroads running to the sea,
and so many stationary girls
whipped off on whirring wheels.

Every Week comes to an end
in men, women and sand—
must keep moving, missing nothing,
climb inconsequential hills,
chew up music without meaning,
come back exhausted to the concrete.

I drink away every Saturday,
never forgetting the prisoner
confined behind cruel walls.
His days no longer have names,
and that murmur, crossing, coursing,
washes round him like a sea,
without his knowing what the wave is,
wave of a humid Saturday.

Oh what exasperating Saturdays,
armed to the teeth with mouths and legs,
unrestrained, in full cry,
drinking past sense—
let us not complain about the babble
not wanting to walk in our company.

SUEÑO DE GATOS

Qué bonito duerme un gato
duerme con patas y peso,
duerme con sus crueles uñas,
y con su sangre sanguinaria,
duerme con todos los anillos
que como círculos quemados
construyeron la geología
de una cola color de arena.

Quisiera dormir como un gato
con todos los pelos del tiempo,
con la lengua del pedernal,
con el sexo seco del fuego
y después de no hablar con nadie,
tenderme sobre todo el mundo,
sobre las tejas y la tierra
intensamente dirigido
a cazar las ratas del sueño.

He visto cómo ondulaba,
durmiendo, el gato: corría
la noche en él como agua oscura,
y a veces se iba a caer,
se iba tal vez a despeñar
en los desnudos ventisqueros,
tal vez creció tanto durmiendo
como un bisabuelo de tigre
y saltaría en las tinieblas
tejados, nubes y volcanes.

Duerme, duerme, gato nocturno
con tus ceremonias de obispo,
y tu bigote de piedra:
ordena todos nuestros sueños,
dirige la oscuridad
de nuestras dormidas proezas
con tu corazón sanguinario
y el largo cuello de tu cola.

CAT'S DREAM

How neatly a cat sleeps,
sleeps with its paws and its substance,
sleeps with its wicked claws,
and with its ruthless blood,
sleeps with all the rings—
a series of burnt circles—
which form the odd geology
of its sand-colored tail.

I should like to sleep like a cat,
with all the fur of time,
with a tongue rough as flint,
with the dry sex of fire;
and after speaking to no one,
stretch myself over the world,
over roofs and landscapes,
with a passionate desire
to hunt the rats in my dreams.

I have seen how the cat asleep
would undulate, how the night
flowed through it like dark water;
and at times, it was going to fall
or possibly plunge into
the bare deserted snowdrifts.
Sometimes it grew so much in sleep
like a tiger's great-grandfather,
and would leap in the darkness over
rooftops, clouds and volcanoes.

Sleep, sleep, cat of the night,
with episcopal ceremony
and your stone-hewn mustache.
Take care of all our dreams;
control the obscurity
of our slumbering prowess
with your relentless heart
and the great ruff of your tail.

VUELVE EL AMIGO

Cuando muere tu amigo
en ti vuelve a morirse.

Te busca hasta encontrarte
para que tú lo mates.

Tomemos nota, andando,
conversando, comiendo,
de su fallecimiento.

Poco importante es lo que le ha pasado.
Todo el mundo sabía sus dolores.
Ya se murió, y apenas se le nombra.
Pasó su nombre y nadie lo detuvo.

Sin embargo él llegó después de muerto
para que sólo aquí lo recordáramos.
Él buscó nuestros ojos implorando.
No lo quisimos ver y no lo vimos.
Entonces ya se fué y ahora no vuelve.
No vuelve más, ya no lo quiere nadie.

THE FRIEND RETURNS

When a friend dies,
in you he returns to die again.

He searches till he finds you
in order for you to kill him.

Let us take note—walking,
eating, talking—
of his dying.

Of little importance is all that has befallen him.
Everyone was well aware of his sorrows.
Now he has died, and he is scarcely mentioned.
His name escaped, and no one clung to it.

Nevertheless, he arrived after his death
so that only here will we remember him.
Imploringly, he tried to catch our eye.
We did not see, nor did we wish to see.
Ultimately, he left, and now does not return,
will not return, with no one wanting him now.

Por qué con esas llamas rojas
se han dispuesto a arder los rubíes?

Por qué el corazón del topacio
tiene panales amarillos?

Por qué se divierte la rosa
cambiando el color de sus sueños?

Por qué se enfría la esmeralda
como una ahogada submarina?

Y por qué palidece el cielo
sobre las estrellas de Junio?

Dónde compra pintura fresca
la cola de la lagartija?

Dónde está el fuego subterráneo
que resucita los claveles?

De dónde saca la sal
esa mirada transparente?

Dónde durmieron los carbones
que se levantaron oscuros?

Y dónde, dónde compra el tigre
rayas de luto, rayas de oro?

Cuándo comenzó a conocer
la madreselva su perfume?

Cuándo se dió cuenta el pino
de su resultado oloroso?

THROUGH A CLOSED MOUTH
THE FLIES ENTER

Why, with those red flames at hand,
have they got ready to burn the rubies?

Why does the heart of the topaz
reveal a yellow honeycomb?

Why does the rose amuse itself
changing the color of its dreams?

Why does the emerald shiver
like a drowned submarine?

Why does the sky grow pale
under the June stars?

Where does the lizard's tail
get its supply of fresh paint?

Where is the underground fire
that revives the carnations?

Where does the salt acquire
the transparency of its glance?

Where did the carbon sleep
that it awoke so dark?

And where, where does the tiger buy
its stripes of mourning, its stripes of gold?

When did the jungle begin
to be aware of its own perfume?

When did the pine tree realize
its own sweet-smelling consequence?

Pablo Neruda / 39

Cuándo aprendieron los limones
la misma doctrina del sol?

Cuándo aprendió a volar el humo?

Cuándo conversan las raíces?

Cómo es el agua en las estrellas?
Por qué el escorpión envenena,
por qué el elefante es benigno?

En qué medita la tortuga?
Dónde se retira la sombra?
Qué canto repite la lluvia?
Dónde van a morir los pájaros?
Y por qué son verdes las hojas?

Es tan poco lo que sabemos
y tanto lo que presumimos
y tan lentamente aprendemos,
que preguntamos, y morimos.
Mejor guardemos orgullo
para la ciudad de los muertos
en el día de los difuntos
y allí cuando el viento recorra
los huecos de tu calavera
te revelará tanto enigma,
susurrándote la verdad
donde estuvieron tus orejas.

When did the lemons learn
the same laws as the sun?

When did smoke learn to fly?

When do roots converse?

How does water reside in stars?
Why is the scorpion poisonous,
the elephant benign?

What is the tortoise brooding on?
Where does shade withdraw to?
What song does the rain repeat?
When are the birds going to die?
And why should leaves be green?

What we know is so little,
and we presume so much,
and learn so slowly
that we ask questions, then die.
Better for us to keep our pride
for the city of the dead
on the day of the departed,
and there, when the wind blows through
the holes in your skull,
it will unveil to you such enigmas,
whispering the truth
through the spaces that were your ears.

BALADA

Vuelve, me dijo una guitarra
cerca de Rancagua, en otoño.
Todos los álamos tenían
color y temblor de campana:
hacía frío y era redondo
el cielo sobre la tristeza.

Entró a la cantina un borracho
tambaleando bajo las uvas
que le llenaban el sombrero
y le salían por los ojos.
Tenía barro en los zapatos,
había pisado la estatua
del otoño y había aplastado
todas sus manos amarillas.

Yo nunca volví a las praderas.
Pero apenas suenan las horas
claudicantes y deshonradas,
cuando al corazón se le caen
los botones y la sonrisa,
cuando dejan de ser celestes
los numerales del olvido,
aquella guitarra me llama,
y ya ha pasado tanto tiempo
que ya tal vez no existe nada,
ni la pradera ni el otoño,
y yo llegaría de pronto
como un fantasma en el vacío
con el sombrero lleno de uvas
preguntando por la guitarra,
y como allí no habría nadie
nadie entendería nada
y yo volvería cerrando
aquella puerta que no existe.

BALLAD

Come back, cried a guitar to me,
near Rancagua, in autumn.
All the poplars wore
the color and tingle of bells.
It was cold, and the sky spread
amply over the sadness.

A drunk came into the canteen,
stumbling under his load of grapes
which filled his hat to the brim
and were coming out of his eyes.
He had mud on his boots.
He had trampled on the effigy
of autumn, and had flattened
all its yellow fingers.

I never went back to the prairies.
But hardly do the hours ring out,
halting and dishonored,
than there falls across my heart
the buttons and the smile;
when they have stopped being benign,
the numerals of forgetting,
that guitar still calls me,
and now so much time has passed
that perhaps nothing exists,
neither the prairie nor the autumn;
and I would arrive, of a sudden,
like a ghost in the great void,
with its hat full of grapes,
asking for a guitar;
and since nobody would be there,
no one would understand anything,
and I would trail back, closing
that door which does not exist.

POR FIN SE FUERON

Todos golpeaban a la puerta
y se llevaban algo mío,
eran gente desconocida
que yo conocía muchísimo,
eran amigos enemigos
que esperaban desconocerme.

Qué podía hacer sin herirlos?

Abrí cajones, llené platos,
destapé versos y botellas:
ellos masticaban con furia
en un comedor descubierto.

Registraban con gran cuidado
los rincones buscando cosas,
yo los encontré durmiendo
varios meses entre mis libros,
mandaban a la cocinera,
caminaban en mis asuntos.

Pero cuando me atormentaron
las brasas de un amor misterioso,
cuando por amor y piedad
padecí dormido y despierto,
la caravana se rompió,
se mudaron con sus camellos.

Se juntaron a maldecirme.
Estos pintorescamente puros
se solazaron, reunidos,
buscando medios con afán
para matarme de algún modo:
el puñal propuso una dama,
el cañón prefirió un valiente,
pero con nocturno entusiasmo
se decidieron por la lengua.

AT LAST THEY HAVE GONE

They all knocked at the door
and carried off something of mine.
They were people who were strangers
but whom I knew very well.
They were friend-enemies
who were waiting to ignore me.

What could I do without hurting them?

I opened drawers, I filled plates,
I uncorked verses and bottles.
They chewed away furiously
in a wide-open dining room.

They took in with extra care
the cubbyholes, looking for things.
I found them fast asleep,
at odd months, among my books.
They gave orders to the cook;
they prowled through my affairs.

But when I was tormented by
the live coals of a mysterious love:
when, through love and true feeling,
I suffered, both sleeping and awake,
the caravan of friends broke up.
They moved off with their camels.

They got together to abuse me.
Those caricatures of virtue
amused themselves, in company,
by zealously looking for ways
of doing me in, somehow:
one woman wanted the dagger,
a braver preferred guns,
but with nightly enthusiasm,
their tongues decided it.

Con intensidad trabajaron,
con ojos, con boca y con manos.
Quién era yo, quién era ella?
Con qué derecho y cuándo y cómo?
Con castos ojos revelaban
interioridades supuestas
y decidían protegerme
contra una incesante vampira.
Adelgazaron gravemente.
Exilados de mi conciencia
se alimentaban con suspiros.

Pasó el tiempo y no estuve solo.

Como siempre en estas historias
mata el amor al enemigo.

Ahora no sé quiénes son:
desapareciendo un minuto
se borraron de mis recuerdos:
son como incómodos zapatos
que al fin me dejaron tranquilo.

Yo estoy con la miel del amor
en la dulzura vespertina.
Se los llevó la sombra a ellos,
malos amigos enemigos,
conocidos desconocidos
que no volverán a mi casa.

They worked with intensity,
with eyes, mouths and hands.
Who was I, who was she?
With what right, and when, and how?
With chaste eyes, they would reveal
family secrets, supposedly,
and would decide to protect me
against a relentless vampire.
They would split hairs so gravely.
In exile from my awareness,
they stuffed themselves on sighs.

The time passed and I was not alone.

As always, in these fairy tales,
love puts the enemy to death.

Now I don't know who they are,
disappearing in a moment,
they scratched themselves from my memory.
They are like uncomfortable shoes
which have finally left me in peace.

Here I am with the honey of love
in the sweetness of evening.
The shadows carried them off,
wretched friend-enemies,
well-known strangers
who will not return to my house.

Como es redondo el mundo
las noches se desploman
y caen hacia abajo.
Y todas se acumulan
y son sólo tinieblas,
abajo, abajo, abajo.

I

Seguí un día cualquiera,
quise saber qué se hacen,
dónde van, dónde mueren.

Por el mar, por las islas,
por ácidas praderas
se perdió, y yo seguía,
escondido detrás
de un árbol o una piedra.

Fué azul, fué anaranjado,
corrió como una rueda,
bajó en la tarde como
bandera de navío,
y más allá en los límites
del silencio y la nieve
se enrolló crepitando
como un hilo de fuego
y se apagó cubierto
por la fría blancura.

II

Las semanas se enrollan,
se hacen nubes, se pierden,
se esconden en el cielo,
allí depositadas
como luz desteñida.

48 / A New Decade (Poems: 1958–1967)

How manifold is the world!
The nights overbalance
and tumble downward.
And all of them accumulate
and are nothing but darknesses:
below below below.

memories bring darkness

I

One day, I followed an odd one.
I wanted to know what they do,
where they go, where they die.

At sea, on the islands,
in the acidic prairies,
it lost itself and I followed,
concealed behind
a tree or a stone.

It was blue, it was orange-tinted,
it ran like a wheel;
it came down in the afternoon like a ship's pennant,
and, further, at the limits
of silence and snow,
it crept, sputtering
like a thread of fire,
and went out, muffled
by the freezing whiteness.

II

The weeks creep past,
form clouds, lose themselves,
conceal themselves in the sky,
abandoned there
like light faded.

Pablo Neruda / 49

Es largo el tiempo, Pedro,
es corto el tiempo, Rosa
y las semanas, justas,
en su papel, gastadas,
se hacinan como granos,
dejan de palpitar.

Hasta que un día el viento
rumoroso, ignorante,
las abre, las extiende
las golpea y ahora
suben como banderas
derrotadas que vuelven
a la patria perdida.

Así son los recuerdos.

Time is long, Pedro.
Time is short, Rosa:
and the weeks, exact
in their roles, used up,
pile up like berries,
stop palpitating.

Till one day, the wind,
rumorous, unaware,
opens them, stretches them,
beats them, and now
they mount like tattered
flags which return
to the lost homeland.

That is the way with memories.

10. *Recomendaciones finales*

Aquí me despido, señores,
después de tantas despedidas
y como no les dejo nada
quiero que todos toquen algo:
lo más inclemente que tuve,
lo más insano y más ferviente
vuelve a la tierra y vuelve a ser:
los pétalos de la bondad
cayeron como campanadas
en la boca verde del viento.

Pero yo recogí con creces
la bondad de amigos y ajenos.
Me recibía la bondad
por donde pasé caminando
y la encontré por todas partes
como un corazón repartido.

Qué fronteras medicinales
no destronaron mi destierro
compartiendo conmigo el pan,
el peligro, el techo y el vino?
El mundo abrió sus arboledas
y entré como Juan por su casa
entre dos filas de ternura.
Tengo en el Sur tantos amigos
como los que tengo en el Norte,
no se puede poner el sol
entre mis amigos del Este,
y cuántos son en el Oeste?
No puedo numerar el trigo.
No puedo nombrar ni contar
los Oyarzunes fraternales:
en América sacudida
por tanta amenaza nocturna

10. *Final Recommendations*

Here I take leave, my friends,
after so many farewells,
and since I leave them nothing,
I want them all to have something;
the most ill-weathered I had,
the maddest, the most rabid,
returns to earth and returns to being.
The petals of gentleness
fell like tolling bell-notes
in the green mouth of the wind.

But abundantly I gathered
the bounty of friends and strangers.
I received my share of plenty
wherever I passed in my travels,
and I found it everywhere
like a shared-out heart.

What medicinal frontiers
kept from overpowering my exile,
sharing bread with me,
danger, shelter, and wine?
The world opened its orchards
and I went in, like Jack to his house,
between twin rows of sympathy.
I have so many friends in the South,
like those I know in the North;
you could not see the sun between
the friends I have in the East,
and how many in the West?
I cannot count ears of wheat.
I cannot number or count
my friends among the Oyarzunes.
In jangling America,
with such nocturnal wanderings,

no hay luna que no me conozca,
ni caminos que no me esperen,
en los pobres pueblos de arcilla
o en las ciudades de cemento
hay algún Arce remoto
que no conozco todavía
pero que nacimos hermanos.

En todas partes recogí
la miel que devoran los osos,
la sumergida primavera,
el tesoro del elefante,
y eso se lo debo a los míos,
a mis parientes cristalinos.
El pueblo me identificó
y nunca dejé de ser pueblo.
Tuve en la palma de la mano
el mundo con sus archipiélagos
y como soy irrenunciable
no renuncié a mi corazón,
a las ostras ni a las estrellas.

De tantas veces que he nacido
tengo una experiencia salobre
como criaturas del mar
con celestiales atavismos
y con destinación terrestre.
Y así me muevo sin saber
a qué mundo voy a volver
o si voy a seguir viviendo.
Mientras se resuelven las cosas
aquí dejé mi testimonio,
mi navegante estravagario
para que leyéndolo mucho
nadie pudiera aprender nada,
sino el movimiento perpetuo
de un hombre claro y confundido,

there is no moon which does not know me,
no roads which do not expect me;
in the poor mud villages
or the concrete cities,
there's a remote Arce*
whom I barely know yet,
except we were born brothers.

Everywhere, I gathered
the honey that bears devour,
the underground spring,
the treasure of the elephant,
and this I owe to my own ones,
to the clarities of my ancestors.
My locality gave me my self
and I have not stopped being local.
I hold in the palm of my hand
the world with its archipelagos,
and since I am not to be renounced,
I did not renounce my heart
to the oysters or the stars.

From so many times of being born,
I keep one salty experience
like creatures of the sea
with their celestial atavism
and with earthly destinations.
Thus I move without knowing
to which world I shall come back
or if I shall go on living.
While things are resolving themselves,
I have left my testament here,
my wandering book of vagaries,
so that reading it over and over,
no one could learn anything
but the perpetual movement
of a man both clear and confused,

---

* A prominent family in Valparaíso.

de un hombre lluvioso y alegre,
enérgico y otoñabundo.

Y ahora detrás de esta hoja
me voy y no desaparezco:
daré un salto en la transparencia
como un nadador del cielo,
y luego volveré a crecer
hasta ser tan pequeño un día
que el viento me llevará
y no sabré cómo me llamo
y no seré cuando despierte:

entonces cantaré en silencio.

of a man both rainy and happy,
boisterous, autumn-rich.

And now I am going behind
this leaf, but not disappearing.
I shall leap in the clear air
like a swimmer in the sky,
and then, come back to growing
until one day I become so small
that the wind will lift me off
and I will not know my name,
and will not exist when I wake.

Then I shall sing in the silence.

For further translations from *Estravagario*, see *Selected Poems of Pablo Neruda*, Edited and translated by Ben Belitt, Introduction by Luis Monguió (New York: Grove Press, 1961), pp. 300–317.

Cien Sonetos de Amor / A Hundred Love Sonnets
1959

Translated by Ben Belitt

MAÑANA

IX

Al golpe de la ola contra la piedra indócil
la claridad estalla y establece su rosa
y el círculo del mar se reduce a un racimo,
a una sola gota de sal azul que cae.

Oh radiante magnolia desatada en la espuma,
magnética viajera cuya muerte florece
y eternamente vuelve a ser y a no ser nada:
sal rota, deslumbrante movimiento marino.

Juntos tú y yo, amor mío, sellamos el silencio,
mientras destruye el mar sus constantes estatuas
y derrumba sus torres de arrebato y blancura,

porque en la trama de estos tejidos invisibles
del agua desbocada, de la incesante arena,
sostenemos la única y acosada ternura.

XII

Plena mujer, manzana carnal, luna caliente,
espeso aroma de algas, lodo y luz machacados,
qué oscura claridad se abre entre tus columnas?
Qué antigua noche el hombre toca con sus sentidos?

Ay, amar es un viaje con agua y con estrellas,
con aire ahogado y bruscas tempestades de harina:
amar es un combate de relámpagos
y dos cuerpos por una sola miel derrotados.

Beso a beso recorro tu pequeño infinito,
tus márgenes, tus ríos, tus pueblos diminutos,
y el fuego genital transformado en delicia

MORNING

The wave's shock on unconsenting stone
splinters your clarity and propagates its rose;
the sea's whole circuit dwindles to a bough,
a single drop of azure churned to brine.

O clear magnolia, unbinding in the spray,
magnetic wanderer dying into flowers,
eternally turned to something turned to nothing,
a salt disaster in the dazzling play of water.

Beloved, ours to seal the silence, yours and mine,
however oceans level their likenesses
and all the towers of rage and pallor totter:

there in the fabric's mesh, unseen by any,
the gout of water and unwearying sand,
all that we thresh in the troubled tenderness is ours.

X I I

Carnal apple, woman incarnate, incandescent moon,
seaweed's sodden aroma, the bog's, and the mash of the light—
what shadowy rigors open between your columns?
What primitive night is touched by a masculine nerve?

Ah, love is a voyage with water and a star,
in drowning air and squalls of precipitate bran;
love is a war of lights in the lightning flashes,
two bodies blasted in a single burst of honey.

Kiss after kiss, I recover your little infinitude,
rivers and shores, your body's diminutive clan,
the genital spark, made dear and delectable,

corre por los delgados caminos de la sangre
hasta precipitarse como un clavel nocturno,
hasta ser y no ser sino un rayo en la sombra.

XIX

Mientras la magna espuma de Isla Negra,
la sal azul, el sol en las olas te mojan,
yo miro los trabajos de la avispa
empeñada en la miel de su universo.

Va y viene equilibrando su recto y rubio vuelo
como si deslizara de un alambre invisible
la elegancia del baile, la sed de su cintura,
y los asesinatos del aguijón maligno.

De petróleo y naranja es su arco iris,
busca como un avión entre la hierba,
con un rumor de espiga vuela, desaparece,

mientras que tú sales del mar, desnuda,
y regresas al mundo llena de sal y sol,
reverberante estatua y espada de la arena.

XXVII

Desnuda eres tan simple como una de tus manos,
lisa, terrestre, mínima, redonda, transparente,
tienes líneas de luna, caminos de manzana,
desnuda eres delgada como el trigo desnudo.

Desnuda eres azul como la noche en Cuba,
tienes enredaderas y estrellas en el pelo,
desnuda eres enorme y amarilla
como el verano en una iglesia de oro.

that races the delicate pathways of your blood,
breaks up from below in a gout of nocturnal carnations
unmaking and making itself, leaving only a glow in the dark.

XIX

There in the towering spumes of Isla Negra
you swim in the blue salt, with the sun on the breakers,
while I follow the machinations of the wasp
who toils in behalf of a universe of honey,

coming and going, point-blank and blond in his poised
levitation, as though tracing invisible wire,
with his dancer's precision, the thirst of his belted abdomen,
intent on the murders that wait in his pitiless needle.

He arches his rainbow in orange and mineral oils,
moves over grass, airborne, like a plane on his mission,
deploys, with a murmur like wind in the wheat, till he vanishes

and I see you again in the sea, mother-naked, emerging,
taking your place in the world, as before, in the sun and the salt,
an echoing presence, like stone, or a rapier blade in the sand.

XXVII

Naked, you are simple as a hand,
minimal, supple, earthy, transparent, round.
The lunar markings, the pathways through the apple,
are yours; naked, you are slender as the wheat.

The Cuban blue of midnight is your color,
naked, I trace stars and tendrils in your skin;
naked, you stand tawny and tremendous,
a summer's wholeness in cathedral gold.

Pablo Neruda / 63

Desnuda eres pequeña como una de tus uñas,
curva, sutil, rosada hasta que nace el día
y te metes en el subterráneo del mundo

como en un largo túnel de trajes de trabajos:
tu claridad se apaga, se viste, se deshoja
y otra vez vuelve a ser una mano desnuda.

XXIX

Vienes de la pobreza de las casas del Sur,
de las regiones duras con frío y terremoto
que cuando hasta sus dioses rodaron a la muerte
nos dieron la lección de la vida en la greda.

Eres un caballito de greda negra, un beso
de barro oscuro, amor, amapola de greda,
paloma del crepúsculo que voló en los caminos,
alcancía con lágrimas de nuestra pobre infancia.

Muchacha, has conservado tu corazón de pobre,
tus pies de pobre acostumbrados a las piedras,
tu boca que no siempre tuvo pan o delicia.

Eres del pobre Sur, de donde viene mi alma:
en su cielo tu madre sigue lavando ropa
con mi madre. Por eso te escogí, compañera.

XXXII

La casa en la mañana con la verdad revuelta
de sábanas y plumas, el origen del día
sin dirección, errante como una pobre barca,
entre los horizontes del orden y del sueño.

Naked, you are tiny as your fingernail;
subtle and curved within the daybreak's pink
you thrust yourself into the subterranean world

a tunnel's length through our duress and clothing:
your clarity trims its flame, unfurls, or covers over,
and again you issue, naked as your hand.

XXIX

You come from the destitute South, from the house
of privation, regions made hard with the earthquake and cold
that gave us hard lessons in living in the chalk and the clay
while the gods whom they worshiped were spinning away to their
    death.

You are a little mare carved in black clay, a kiss
dusky with pitch, beloved, a clay poppy,
a pigeon of twilight that fluttered its way on the roads
and followed us into a childhood of want, with its tears.

You who always preserved your heart's poverty,
girl with the feet of the needy, accustomed to stones,
whose mouth was not always acquainted with sweetmeat and
    bread:

You come from the destitute South that once nurtured my soul;
in her heaven, your mother goes on washing clothes
with my mother. Therefore I have singled you out to be my
    companion.

XXXII

Morning in the house: the truth is ours again,
feathers and linens, the sources of a day
intent on nothing, a leaky barge adrift
within a double skyline: dream and order.

Pablo Neruda / 65

Las cosas quieren arrastrar vestigios,
adherencias sin rumbo, herencias frías,
los papeles esconden vocales arrugadas
y en la botella el vino quiere seguir su ayer.

Ordenadora, pasas vibrando como abeja
tocando las regiones perdidas por la sombra
conquistando la luz con tu blanca energía.

Y se construye entonces la claridad de nuevo:
obedecen las cosas al viento de la vida
y el orden establece su pan y su paloma.

MEDIODÍA

XXXV

Tu mano fué volando de mis ojos al día.
Entró la luz como un rosal abierto.
Arena y cielo palpitaban como una
culminante colmena cortada en las turquesas.

Tu mano tocó sílabas que tintineaban, copas,
alcuzas con aceites amarillos,
corolas, manantiales y, sobre todo, amor,
amor: tu mano pura preservó las cucharas.

La tarde fué. La noche deslizó sigilosa
sobre el sueño del hombre su cápsula celeste.
Un triste olor salvaje soltó la madreselva.

Y tu mano volvió de su vuelo volando
a cerrar su plumaje que yo creí perdido
sobre mis ojos devorados por la sombra.

XXXVIII

Tu casa suena como un tren a mediodía,
zumban las avispas, cantan las cacerolas,

Things root in their rubbish, in search of their vestiges—
a clinging jetsam going nowhere, unloved bequests,
a papery noise of hidden corrugations,
dregs in a bottle in search of the night before.

Dear Orderer, who moves with a passing bee's pulsation,
it is for you to touch the vanishing realm of shadow
and force your way to the light, with the power of white.

Definition returns in you: all is rebuilt again,
the things of the wind respond to the life of the world
and order apportions its dove and its daily bread.

AFTERNOON

XXXV

All day I saw your flying hand before me.
Light flooded in, a tree of opening roses.
Sand and sky vibrated like a hive
with all its waxes packed under turquoise facets.

Your touch made syllables tinkle, cups and glasses,
cruets of oil and oleaginous golds,
corollas and the wellsprings of the world—above all, love:
in love, your pure hand kept its watch upon the spoons.

Till it was evening. Night's cunning closed the human
dreamer into the bubble of its heaven.
An odor, savage and sad, leapt from the honeysuckle.

But your flying hand kept flying; your hand flew on,
while every feather lost to my sight till then,
shut on my ravaged vision, and vision darkened.

XXXVIII

Your house has the sound of a train in the afternoon:
a buzzing of wasps, a singing of casseroles;

Pablo Neruda / 67

la cascada enumera los hechos del rocío,
tu risa desarrolla su trino de palmera.

La luz azul del muro conversa con la piedra,
llega como un pastor silbando un telegrama
y entre las dos higueras de voz verde
Homero sube con zapatos sigilosos.

Sólo aquí la ciudad no tiene voz ni llanto,
ni sin fin, ni sonatas, ni labios, ni bocina
sino un discurso de cascada y de leones,

y tú que subes, cantas, corres, caminas, bajas,
plantas, coses, cocinas, clavas, escribes, vuelves,
o te has ido y se sabe que comenzó el invierno.

XL

Era verde el silencio, mojada era la luz,
temblaba el mes de Junio como una mariposa
y en el austral dominio, desde el mar y las piedras,
Matilde, atravesaste el mediodía.

Ibas cargada de flores ferruginosas,
algas que el viento sur atormenta y olvida,
aún blancas, agrietadas por la sal devorante,
tus manos levantaban las espigas de arena.

Amo tus dones puros, tu piel de piedra intacta,
tus uñas ofrecidas en el sol de tus dedos,
tu boca derramada por toda la alegría

pero, para mi casa vecina del abismo,
dame el atormentado sistema del silencio,
el pabellón del mar olvidado en la arena.

the waterfall totals the sum of the dew's occupation,
and your laugh runs the trills of the palm tree's coloratura.

An azure light in the wall babbles on with the stone,
it comes with a whistle like a shepherd bringing telegrams;
between the double flame of the bonfire and the sounding green
Homer ascends on his surreptitious sandals.

Only here can a city live without woe or vociferation,
uneternal, without bugles or lips or sonatas,
with only a dialog of lions and falling water,

while you move upward or down on the stairs, walking or running,
singing or planting, sewing or cooking or nailing things down,
writing, returning; or gone: when all the world says: It is winter.

XL

A stillness gone green, with the light showing watery,
a month trembled by like a butterfly: June. All the while
you were there on the southernmost reaches, Matilda, traversing
the midday's dominion, the limits of ocean and stone.

You went bearing your cargo of ferruginous flowers,
seaweed lashed up by squalls from the South, and forgotten,
livid with salt and cracked open by the passing devourer,
lifted high in your hands like stalks in a wheatfield of sand.

And I, who adore those pure bounties, your skin's stone integrity,
your fingernails rayed open for all in a sunburst of fingers,
your mouth welling up its delight without stint or exception,

must ask in behalf of a house I have built on the edges'
abysses, something more: the agonist's system of silence
and the ocean's tormented pavilions left behind in the sand.

Desdichas del mes de Enero cuando el indiferente
mediodía establece su ecuación en el cielo,
un oro duro como el vino de una copa colmada
llena la tierra hasta sus límites azules.

Desdichas de este tiempo parecidas a uvas
pequeñas que agruparon verde amargo,
confusas, escondidas lágrimas de los días
hasta que la intemperie publicó sus racimos.

Sí, gérmenes, dolores, todo lo que palpita
aterrado, a la luz crepitante de Enero,
madurará, arderá como ardieron los frutos.

Divididos serán los pesares: el alma
dará un golpe de viento, y la morada
quedará limpia con el pan fresco en la mesa.

Aquí está el pan, el vino, la mesa, la morada:
el menester del hombre, la mujer y la vida:
a este sitio corría la paz vertiginosa,
por esta luz ardió la común quemadura.

Honor a tus dos manos que vuelan preparando
los blancos resultados del canto y la cocina,
salve! la integridad de tus pies corredores
viva! la bailarina que baila con la escoba.

Aquellos bruscos ríos con aguas y amenazas,
aquel atormentado pabellón de la espuma,
aquellos incendiarios panales y arrecifes

son hoy este reposo de tu sangre en la mía,
este cauce estrellado y azul como la noche,
esta simplicidad sin fin de la ternura.

The unlucky turns of January, when an indifferent
midday establishes its equation in the sky,
an unbreakable gold like wine in the rim of a cup
brimming the span of the earth to its bluest horizon.

The unlucky turns of a season, crowding its clusters
like hard little grapes packed in acidulous green,
a long day's secretive weeping, confusion and tears,
until all is revealed in the storm cloud's opening branches.

Yes: the seeds and the travail, all that shudders below
underfoot, underground, in the crackling January light—
ripeness is all, and will burn in the burnish of fruits.

To each in his time the woes of the world; yet the spirit
will beat with the fists of the wind, and the whole habitation
of man will be cleansed, with bread newly baked for the table.

LIII

Here is the bread and the wine, the table, the shelter:
all of man's ministry, woman's work and our lives':
the vertiginous peace of the world flows down to this place
and under this light the blaze of the commonwealth burns.

Praise to the hands, your flying hands, making ready
the consummate whiteness of song and the white of the kitchen;
praise to your flying feet and your footstep's integrity,
vivas and praise to the dancer dancing on with the broom.

All those barbarous rivers compounding a menace of waters,
the exacerbate pavilion in the spume,
the incendiary combs of honey and the reefs,

are now made one—your blood's repose and mine,
this watershed of midnight blues and stars,
this tenderness made simple, world without end.

Pablo Neruda / 71

TARDE

A ti te hiere aquel que quiso hacerme daño,
y el golpe del veneno contra mí dirigido
como por una red pasa entre mis trabajos
y en ti deja una mancha de óxido y desvelo.

No quiero ver, amor, en la luna florida
de tu frente cruzar el odio que me acecha.
No quiero que en tu sueño deje el rencor ajeno
olvidada su inútil corona de cuchillos.

Donde voy van detrás de mí pasos amargos,
donde río una mueca de horror copia mi cara,
donde canto la envidia maldice, ríe y roe.

Y es ésa, amor, la sombra que la vida me ha dado:
es un traje vacío que me sigue cojeando
como un espantapájaros de sonrisa sangrienta.

L X V I I I

(Mascarón de Proa)

La niña de madera no llegó caminando:
allí de pronto estuvo sentada en los ladrillos,
viejas flores del mar cubrían su cabeza,
su mirada tenía tristeza de raíces.

Allí quedó mirando nuestras vidas abiertas,
el ir y ser y andar y volver por la tierra,
el día destiñendo sus pétalos graduales.
Vigilaba sin vernos la niña de madera.

La niña coronada por las antiguas olas,
allí miraba con sus ojos derrotados:
sabía que vivimos en una red remota

EVENING

Whoever intends me harm, lets your blood, too:
the poisonous blow directed against me,
falling across my labors like a net,
darkens your wincing flesh in its corrosion.

Under a flowering moon, beloved, may I never
see the odium of others lining your forehead,
remote or forgotten rancors ravage your sleep
with their useless crown of knives: I do not wish to see it.

Behind me as I move, the malevolent pass,
a grimacing horror copies my face if I laugh,
I sing among mockers and backbiters, cursed by the covetous.

This is my life, my darling, the cloud life has gathered me under,
the vacuous garment that limps at my heels as I go,
the scarecrow smiling his bloody smile among the crows.

L X V I I I

(Figurehead)

The girl in the wood never came this way by foot:
all at once she was there in her place, on her dais of bricks,
the primordial flowers of the ocean crowding her head,
bemused, with the unwavering gaze of those who remember their
    roots.

And remained in that place, caught in our manifest lives
—our goings and comings, the being and fading of the things
of the earth, while daylight distended its gradual petals.
The girl in the wood saw each of us, and saw nothing.

The girl with the wreath of antediluvian waves,
saw everything pass in that place, with her ruining eyes,
looked into the ambiguous net where we live out our lives,

Pablo Neruda / 73

de tiempo y agua y olas y sonidos y lluvia,
sin saber si existimos o si somos su sueño.
Ésta es la historia de la muchacha de madera.

LXXVI

Diego Rivera con la paciencia del oso
buscaba la esmeralda del bosque en la pintura
o el bermellón, la flor súbita de la sangre,
recogía la luz del mundo en tu retrato.

Pintaba el imperioso traje de tu nariz,
la centella de tus pupilas desbocadas,
tus uñas que alimentan la envidia de la luna,
y en tu piel estival, tu boca de sandía.

Te puso dos cabezas de volcán encendidas
por fuego, por amor, por estirpe araucana,
y sobre los dos rostros dorados de la greda

te cubrió con el casco de un incendio bravío
y allí secretamente quedaron enredados
mis ojos en su torre total: tu cabellera.

LXXVII

Hoy es hoy con el peso de todo el tiempo ido,
con las alas de todo lo que será mañana,
hoy es el Sur del mar, la vieja edad del agua
y la composición de un nuevo día.

A tu boca elevada a la luz o a la luna
se agregaron los pétalos de un día consumido,
y ayer viene trotando por su calle sombría
para que recordemos su rostro que se ha muerto.

knotted with time and the water, the waves, the cries and the
    rain,
never knowing if we live in our selves, or are part of her dream.
A tale of a girl in the wood: this is her fable.

L X X V I

Diego Rivera, with the patience of a bear,
hunted the emerald in the forest of his art,
the blood's spontaneous blossom of vermilion,
rifling a world of light to fix your likeness.

He painted the imperial drapery of your nose,
your pupils' opulent thunderbolt, the bosses
on your fingernails that widen the envious moon,
and there in the summer of your skin, your mouth like
    watermelons.

He painted you double-headed, each way a volcano kindled,
brilliant with passion and flame, your Araucanian kin;
and over the twofold faces and the clayey gold,

he covered your head in the helmet's hot emblazoning
tangled with secretive leafage, where my eyes
keep watch in the covert of their total tower: your hair.

L X X V I I

Today is today, with the total weight of time
passed, and winged with what will be tomorrow;
today is the Southern ocean, the antiquities
of water, and the new day's changing order.

Circling your mouth upturned to the sunlight or moon,
the petals of yesterday's phases cluster their masses,
while yesterday travels your darkening streets, at a canter,
to bring us your face's death, the better to be remembered.

Pablo Neruda / 75

Hoy, ayer y mañana se comen caminando,
consumimos un día como una vaca ardiente,
nuestro ganado espera con sus días contados,

pero en tu corazón el tiempo echó su harina,
mi amor construyó un horno con barro de Temuco:
tú eres el pan de cada día para mi alma.

LXXVIII

No tengo nunca más, no tengo siempre. En la arena
la victoria dejó sus pies perdidos.
Soy un pobre hombre dispuesto a amar a sus semejantes.
No sé quién eres. Te amo. No doy, no vendo espinas.

Alguien sabrá tal vez que no tejí coronas
sangrientas, que combatí la burla,
y que en verdad llené la pleamar de mi alma.
Yo pagué la vileza con palomas.

Yo no tengo jamás porque distinto
fuí, soy, seré. Y en nombre
de mi cambiante amor proclamo la pureza.

La muerte es sólo piedra del olvido.
Te amo, beso en tu boca la alegría.
Traigamos leña. Haremos fuego en la montaña.

NOCHE

LXXXV

Del mar hacia las calles corre la vaga niebla
como el vapor de un buey enterrado en el frío,
y largas lenguas de agua se acumulan cubriendo
el mes que a nuestras vidas prometió ser celeste.

76 / A New Decade (Poems: 1958–1967)

Today, tomorrow, yesterday, destroy themselves in passing:
we feast on the fat of the day like a cow on a spit,
while our counted flock stands idle in the tally of days;

but elsewhere, under your heart, times empties its grains
while my love builds its ovens of clay with Temuco adobe
and you nourish my soul with your bounty of daily bread.

LXXVIII

Never, forever . . . they do not concern me. Victory's
footstep printing the sands avails us nothing.
I live, a bedeviled man, disposed, like any other,
to cherish my human affinities. Whoever you are, I love you.

The peddling and plaiting of thorns is not my concern, and many
    know
this. I am no weaver of bloody crowns. I fought with the frivolous
and the tide of my spirit runs full; and in sober earnest,
my detractors are paid in full with a volley of doves.

Never is no part of me; because I am I with
a difference: was, and will always be so; and I speak
for the pureness of things in the name of my love's metamorphoses.

Death is the stone into which our oblivion hardens.
I love you. I kiss happiness into your lips. Let us
gather up sticks for a fire. Let us kindle a fire on the mountains.

NIGHT

LXXXV

The insubstantial fog seeps toward the streets from the ocean,
an ox's breath in the burial mound of the cold,
while lengthening tongues of the water cover over
a month that promised so much for our lives: celestial
    consummation.

Pablo Neruda / 77

Adelantado otoño, panal silbante de hojas,
cuando sobre los pueblos palpita tu estandarte
cantan mujeres locas despidiendo a los ríos,
los caballos relinchan hacia la Patagonia.

Hay una enredadera vespertina en tu rostro
que crece silenciosa por el amor llevada
hasta las herraduras crepitantes del cielo.

Me inclino sobre el fuego de tu cuerpo nocturno
y no sólo tus senos amo sino el otoño
que esparce por la niebla su sangre ultramarina.

LXXXVI

Oh Cruz del Sur, oh trébol de fósforo fragante,
con cuatro besos hoy penetró tu hermosura
y atravesó la sombra y mi sombrero:
la luna iba redonda por el frío.

Entonces con mi amor, con mi amada, oh diamantes
de escarcha azul, serenidad del cielo,
espejo, apareciste y se llenó la noche
con tus cuatro bodegas temblorosas de vino.

Oh palpitante plata de pez pulido y puro,
cruz verde, perejil de la sombra radiante,
luciérnaga a la unidad del cielo condenada,

descansa en mí, cerremos tus ojos y los míos.
Por un minuto duerme con la noche del hombre.
Enciende en mí tus cuatro números constelados.

LXXXVII

Las tres aves del mar, tres rayos, tres tijeras,
cruzaron por el cielo frío hacia Antofagasta,
por eso quedó el aire tembloroso,
todo tembló como bandera herida.

An untimely autumn, with a sibilant panel of leaves
that breaks out its quivering color over villages
where idiot girls sing their farewells to the rivers
and the horses' whinny drifts toward Patagonia.

In evening's thicket, I see the entanglements climbing
your face, tendrils crowding the silence that love
lifted heavenward, toward the horseshoes of sputtering iron.

I bend toward the bonfires of your nocturnal body,
seeking your breast in love, and loving the autumn
that spends the ultramarine of your blood on the scattering mist.

LXXXVI

Southern Cross, trefoil of aromatic phosphor,
today your beauty struck with its fourfold kiss, a bolt
driven into the darkness and out again through my hat,
while the moon widened its circumference in the cold.

My love and my beloved followed you there—diamonds
of frosty blue in the serenity of heaven,
looking glasses; you appeared and the night grew enormous:
four wine cellars in air, tremulous with wine.

Pure fish of space, quicksilver, incandescent,
green cross or parsley light in the dark,
firefly fixed in the singleness of heaven,

rest here with me, too, let us darken our eyelids together.
Sleep in the night of the human, for a passing minute only.
Blazon my body with your four zodiacal numbers.

LXXXVII

Three sea birds, three lightning flashes, three flying scissors
crossed the cold heavens toward Antofagasta:
that is what troubled the air, leaving everything tremulous,
that's why the universe shook like a banner in rags.

Pablo Neruda / 79

Soledad, dame el signo de tu incesante origen,
el apenas camino de los pájaros crueles,
y la palpitación que sin duda precede
a la miel, a la música, al mar, al nacimiento.

(Soledad sostenida por un constante rostro
como una grave flor sin cesar extendida
hasta abarcar la pura muchedumbre del cielo.)

Volaban alas frías del mar, del Archipiélago,
hacia la arena del Noroeste de Chile.
Y la noche cerró su celeste cerrojo.

XC

Pensé morir, sentí de cerca el frío,
y de cuanto viví sólo a ti te dejaba:
tu boca era mi día y mi noche terrestres
y tu piel la república fundada por mis besos.

En ese instante se terminaron los libros,
la amistad, los tesoros sin tregua acumulados,
la casa transparente que tú y yo construímos:
todo dejó de ser, menos tus ojos.

Porque el amor, mientras la vida nos acosa,
es simplemente una ola alta sobre las olas,
pero ay cuando la muerte viene a tocar la puerta

hay sólo tu mirada para tanto vacío,
sólo tu claridad para no seguir siendo,
sólo tu amor para cerrar la sombra.

XCVIII

Y esta palabra, este papel escrito
por las mil manos de una sola mano,
no queda en ti, no sirve para sueños,
cae a la tierra: allí se continúa.

80 / A New Decade (Poems: 1958–1967)

Solitude, give me a sign: show your perpetual origin,
the probable lanes through the air for the pitiless birds,
the pulsation that beats, incontestably, a moment before
the honey is spilt, or the music, the birth-breach, the ocean.

(That solitude poised in a face's eternity,
that saturnine flower incessantly spreading its petals,
till heaven's immaculate legions are closed in a span.)

Cold wings blowing in from the sea, from the ringed
Archipelago, northeast to the deserts of Chile.
The night turns its key in the lock and the zodiac closes.

X C

I dreamed that I died: that I felt the cold close to me;
and all that was left of my life was contained in your presence:
your mouth was the daylight and dark of my world,
your skin, the republic I shaped for myself with my kisses.

Straightway, the books of the world were all ended,
all friendships, all treasures restlessly cramming the vaults,
the diaphanous house that we built for a lifetime together—
all ceased to exist, till nothing remained but your eyes.

So long as we live, or as long as a lifetime's vexation,
love is a breaker thrown high on the breakers' successions;
but when death in its time chooses to pummel the doors—

Ay! there is only your face to fill up the vacancy,
only your clarity pressing back on the whole of non-being,
only your love, where the dark of the world closes in.

X C V I I I

The word set down, this scribbling on the paper
by all the thousand hands of my one hand,
will not survive in you, or accommodate your dreaming:
it drops to earth, and there it is continued.

Pablo Neruda / 81

No importa que la luz o la alabanza
se derramen y salgan de la copa
si fueron un tenaz temblor del vino,
si se tiñó tu boca de amaranto.

No quiere más la sílaba tardía,
lo que trae y retrae el arrecife
de mis recuerdos, la irritada espuma,

no quiere más sino escribir tu nombre.
Y aunque lo calle mi sombrío amor
más tarde lo dirá la primavera.

Whatever the light and adulation spill
from the passing cup that runneth over—it cannot matter
so long as all works strongly in the wine
and stains your mouth an amaranthine color.

Even the tardy syllable has ceased to treasure
all that the reefs of my remembrance gathered
and regathered, the exacerbated spume:

its simple passion is: to write your name.
And however much love's darkness stifles it,
the spring will speak it plainly in due time.

Las Piedras de Chile / The Stones of Chile
1961

Translated by Ben Belitt

SOME WORDS FOR A BOOK OF STONES

This flinty book, born in the desolate coastlands and mountain ranges of my country, has lived twenty years in my mind . . . The poet must sing with his countrymen and endow all mankind with all that pertains to being a man: living and dreaming, light and dark, reason and vagary. But let us never lose sight of the stones! We ought never forget those taciturn castles, the contours and bristling largesse of the planet. They fortify citadels, push toward extinction or murder, embellish existence but extenuate nothing, preserve to the end the secret of ultraterrestrial matter, independent, eternal. My compatriot, Gabriela Mistral, used to say: *In Chile, it is the skeletal one sees first of all, the profusion of rock in the mountains and sand.* . . . I first came to Isla Negra in 1939: the whole coastland was sown with those portentous presences in stone which I later transformed into a hoarse and soaking language, a jumble of watery cries and primordial intimations. This book, adorned with the pictures of creaturely rocks, is a conversation open to poets all over the earth who seek to encompass and encounter the secret of rock and of life.

P.N.

LA GRAN MESA DE PIEDRA DURA

A la mesa de piedra llegamos
los niños de Lota, de Quepe,
de Quitratúe, de Metrenco,
de Ranquilco, de Selva Oscura,
de Yumbel, de Yungay, de Osorno.

Nos sentamos junto a la mesa,
a la mesa fría del mundo,
y no nos trajo nadie nada,
todo se había terminado,
se lo habían comido todo.

Un solo plato está esperando
sobre la inmensa mesa dura,
del mundo y su vasto vacío:
y todavía un niño espera,
él es la verdad de los sueños,
él es la esperanza terrestre.

THE GREAT ROCK TABLE

We come to the stone table together
all the children of Lota and Quepe,
Quitratúe, Metrenco,
Ranquilco, the Dark Forest,
Yumbel, Yungay and Osorno.

We take our places at the table together,
the world's chilly trenchermen,
but no one comes forth with the feast:
the great supper is eaten
and the guests left no crumb on the stones.

One platter alone remains
on the table's tremendous opacity,
the infinite void and the world:
one child still waits for his portion,
the child that is truth in a dream
and the faith of the earth.

EL ARPA

Iba sola la música. No había pluma, pelo,
leche, humo, nombres, no era noche ni día,
sola entre los planetas naciendo del eclipse
la música temblaba como una vestidura.
De pronto el fuego, el frío cuajaron una gota
y plasmó el universo su extenso escaparate,
lava, ceniza hirsuta, resbaladiza aurora,
todo fué trasmigrando de dureza en dureza
y bajo la humedad recién celeste
estableció el diamante su helada simetría.
Entonces el sonido primordial,
la solitaria música del mundo
se congeló y cayó convertida en estrella,
en arpa, en cítara, en silencio, en piedra.

Por la costa de Chile, con frío, y en invierno,
cuando cae la lluvia lavando las semanas,
oíd: la soledad vuelve a ser música,
y no sé, me parece, que el aire, que la lluvia,
que el tiempo, algo con ola y alas,
pasa, crece. Y el arpa despierta del olvido.

THE HARP

Only the music moved. Milks, feathers, skins,
numbers and smoke—nothing else was, neither night
nor the day, as the planets emerged from the music's
eclipse to a rustle of music like drapery.
All at once hot and cold curdled into a drop,
the great press of the universe took form
in the lava, a mane in the ashes, dawn slithering down,
hardness transfigured itself into hardness
under the drizzle that once was a part of the sky,
as the diamond conceived its symmetrical frieze in the snow.
Sound grew primordial then,
a world's lonely music
congealing and plunging and trying its changes: the meteor's
shape, shapes of the harp and the zither, the silence, the stone.

Chile's great seaboard, frozen into its winter,
washes the weeks in the rain.
Listen: that solitude turning to music again
as all seems to widen and fail past my knowing—
air, time, and the rains, a thing in the waves and the feathers.
And oblivion wakes for the harp.

LA ESTATUA CIEGA

Hace mil veces mil
años de piedra
yo fuí picapedrero
y esto fué lo que hice,
golpeando
sin manos
ni martillo,
abriendo
sin cincel,
mirando el sol sin ojos,
sin ser,
sin existir sino en el viento,
sin otro pensamiento que una ola,
sin otras herramientas
que el tiempo,
el tiempo,
el tiempo.

Hice la estatua ciega
que no mirara,
que allí
en la desolada
arena
mantuviera su mole
como mi monumento:
la estatua
ciega
que aquel primer hombre
que salió de la piedra,
el hijo de la fuerza,
el primero
que cavó, tocó, impuso
su creación perdida,
buscó el fuego.

Y así nací, desnudo
y azul picapedrero,

BLIND STATUE

A millennium ago and a thousand
times in the stone,
I slashed at the flint
to accomplish this marvel:
I struck
without hammer
or hands,
pierced
without chisel,
stared into the sun without eyes
or identity,
a whim of the wind,
with only a wave for my thought
and time for a tool
time passing,
time passing.

I hewed the blind statue
that looks out at nothing
and nurtures
its mass
like a
monument
there in the sand's desolation:
the blind
work
of that first of the movers
to step from the rock,
assiduity's child,
the first
gouger and toucher to force from the flint
his fleeting creation
and forage for fire.

Naked and blue, I was born
to myself, a stonecutter

a lo largo de costas en tinieblas,
de ríos aún oscuros,
en cuevas azotadas por la cola
de los saurios sombríos
y me costó encontrarme,
hacerme manos,
ojos, dedos, buscar
mi propia sangre,
y entonces mi alegría
se hizo estatua:
mi propia forma que copié golpeando
a través de los siglos en la piedra.

on a shadowy seacoast, adrift
on the parallel dark of the rivers,
in caverns lashed by the tail
of the taciturn saurians.
It was hard to encompass myself,
devise hands,
fingers and eyes for myself, probe
for the blood that was mine;
but I cut through the stone
of my joy toward the statue,
the effigy shaped like myself, hacked
in the rock and the centuries.

LA TORTUGA

La tortuga que
anduvo
tanto tiempo
y tanto vió
con
sus
antiguos
ojos,
la tortuga
que comió
aceitunas
del más profundo
mar,
la tortuga que nadó
siete siglos
y conoció
siete
mil
primaveras,
la tortuga
blindada
contra
el calor
y el frío,
contra
los rayos y las olas,
la tortuga
amarilla
y plateada,
con severos
lunares
ambarinos
y pies de rapiña,
la tortuga
se quedó
aquí
durmiendo,
y no lo sabe.

THE TURTLE

The turtle
toiling forward
so long,
having seen so much
with
his
antediluvian
eyes:
the turtle,
munching
olives
where the ocean is
deepest:
the turtle that swam
seven centuries
and knew
seven
millennial
springs:
the turtle
hooded
against
hot
and cold,
against
comber and glitter:
the yellowing
turtle,
plated
with hard
moonmarks
of amber
and the feet of a predator:
the turtle
sleeps
now, having
come to a halt,
hardly aware of it.

De tan vieja
se fué
poniendo dura,
dejó
de amar las olas
y fué rígida
como una plancha de planchar.
Cerró
los ojos que
tanto
mar, cielo, tiempo y tierra
desafiaron,
y se durmió
entre las otras
piedras.

Patriarch, long
hardening
into his time,
he grew
weary of waves
and stiffened himself
like a flatiron.
Having dared
so much
ocean and sky, time and terrain,
he let his eyes droop
and then slept,
a boulder
among other boulders.

Las piedrecitas puras,
olivas ovaladas,
fueron antes
población
de las viñas
del océano,
racimos agrupados,
uvas de los panales
sumergidos:
la ola las desgranaba,
caían en el viento,
rodaban al abismo abismo abismo
entre lentos pescados,
sonámbulas medusas,
colas de lacerantes tiburones,
corvinas como balas!
las piedras transparentes,
las suavísimas piedras,
piedrecitas,
resbalaron
hacia el fondo del húmedo reinado,
más abajo, hacia donde
sale otra vez el cielo
y muere el mar sobre sus alcachofas.
Rodaron y rodaron
entre dedos y labios submarinos
hasta la suavidad inacabable,
hasta ser sólo tacto,
curva de copa suave,
pétalo de cadera.
Entonces arreció la marejada
y un golpe de ola dura,
una mano de piedra
aventó los guijarros,
los desgranó en la costa
y allí en silencio desaparecieron:
pequeños dientes de ámbar,

STONES FOR MARIA

These perfect pebbles,
olives in ovals,
once were
vineyards
that peopled
the ocean,
clustering branches,
grapes combed from the underseas
hives:
threshed fine by the waves
and felled by the wind,
they circled the abysses' abysses' abysses
among the unhurrying fins and
sleepwalking jellyfish
the flail in the tail of the shark,
the eels' fusillades.
Diaphanous stones,
sleek stones,
little pebbles—all
veered
toward the humid dominions,
shunted below in the depths
where the sky re-emerges, and the sea
dies in the artichokes.
Circling and circling,
among subterranean fingers and lips,
they touched that apotheosis
of the suave where only the tactile remains,
the curve in the smooth of the cup
and the flank of the petal.
It was then that the sea-swell compounded
its powers in a hard shock of water,
a fist in the stone,
winnowed the cobbles
and sifted the beaches
till all disappeared in the silence:
the small teeth of amber,

Pablo Neruda / 101

pasas de miel y sal, porotos de agua,
aceitunas azules de la ola,
almendras olvidadas de la arena. . . .

raisins of honey and salt, watery peapods,
blue olives packing the waves,
almonds, abandoned in sand . . .

AL AIRE EN LA PIEDRA

En la peña desnuda
y en el pelo
aire
de piedra y ola.
Todo cambió de piel hora por hora.
La sal fué luz salada,
el mar abrió
sus nubes,
el cielo
despeñó su espuma verde:
como una flor
clavada en una
lanza de oro
el día resplandece:
todo
es
campana, copa,
vacío que se eleva,
corazón transparente,
piedra
y
agua.

AIR IN THE STONE

In the stripped stone
and the hairs of my head
airs move
from the rock and the wave.
Hour after hour, that changing of skins,
the salt in the light's marination.
The sea opened
clouds,
the sky
flung its green spray:
day glitters
like a flower
driven into the gold
of a lance:
all
is a lifting of
bells, cups,
and vacancy,
the heart's whole transparency
in
the boulder,
the water.

LA NAVE

Íbamos y subíamos: el mundo
era un sediento mediodía,
no temblaba el aire, no existían las hojas,
el agua estaba lejos.

La nave o proa entonces
surgió de los desiertos,
navegaba hacia el cielo:
una punta de piedra dirigida
hacia el insoportable infinito,
una basílica cerrada
por los dioses perdidos
y allí estaba la proa, flecha o nave
o torre tremebunda,
y para la fatiga,
la sed, la polvorienta,
la sudorosa estirpe
del hombre que subía
las cordilleras duras,
ni agua ni pan ni pasto,
sólo una roca grande que subía,
sólo la nave dura de la piedra y la música.

Hasta cuándo? grité, gritamos.
Ya nos mató la madrecita tierra
con su cactus férreo,
con su maternidad ferruginosa,
con todo este desierto,
sudor, viento y arena,
y cuando ya llegábamos
a descansar envueltos en vacío
una nave de piedra
quería aún embarcarnos
hacia donde sin alas
no se puede volar
sin haber muerto.

THE SHIP

We climbed up, we pressed on. The parched
world stood at midday,
not a tremor of air, not a leaf,
and the water so distant.

It was then that the ship, or a ship's prow
hove to on the desert,
sailing into the sky:
a flint pinpoint aimed
at the unbearable infinite,
a basilica closed
by the perishing gods:
there was the bowsprit, the ship, the arrowhead,
the grueling tower,
and for our weariness,
thirst, the dust-laden
sweat, the mark
of the men who climb the hard uplands
—neither water, nor pasture, nor bread,
only a great rock arising,
a hard ship of stone; and that music.

How much farther, we cried: little world,
I cried out, little mother, you murder us all
with the cactus's iron,
we fail in your iron maternity,
all is wilderness,
sweat, wind, and sand;
and even when we paused in the interval
in the circle of vacancy,
the stone ship
stood ready to open its hold to us there,
force us forward, unwinged,
to the regions where nothing flies up
without suffering death.

Esto pasó cuando íbamos cansados
y la cordillera era dura,
pesada como una cadena.

Sólo hasta allí llegó mi viaje:
más allá empezaba la muerte.

Dog-tired we were, then,
the ring of the ranges was hard,
and heavy the links of the chain.

But the voyage led me no farther:
death began in the distance.

Allí termina todo
y no termina:
allí comienza todo:
se despiden los ríos en el hielo,
el aire se ha casado con la nieve,
no hay calles ni caballos
y el único edificio
lo construyó la piedra.
Nadie habita el castillo
ni las almas perdidas
que frío y viento frío
amedrentaron:
es sola allí la soledad del mundo,
y por eso la piedra
se hizo música,
elevó sus delgadas estaturas,
se levantó para gritar o cantar
pero se quedó muda.
Sólo el viento,
el látigo
del Polo Sur que silba,
sólo el vacío blanco
y un sonido de pájaros de lluvia
sobre el castillo de la soledad.

STONES OF ANTARCTICA

Here the interminable
ends: here
all things begin:
the river's farewell in the ice,
the marriage of air and the snow.
The streets and the horses are nowhere:
only the stone's fabrications
remain.
No one lives at the castle,
the lost apparitions
have been frightened away
by the cold and the wind's bitterness:
it is this
that gave song to the stone
and suspended its delicate semblances
heaved up like a cry or a tune
and kept mute to the end.
Only the wind stays,
the hiss
in the whip of the South Pole,
only the white of the emptiness,
bird-sounds in the rain
over a castle of solitude.

Es así en esta costa.
De pronto, retorcidas,
acerbas, hacinadas,
estáticos
derrumbes
o tenaces teatros,
naves y galerías
o rodantes
muñones cercenados:
es así en esta costa
el lunar roquerío,
las uvas del granito.

Manchas anaranjadas
de óxido, vetas verdes,
sobre la paz calcárea
que golpea la espuma con sus llaves
o el alba con su rosa
y son así estas piedras:
nadie sabe
si salieron del mar o al mar regresan,
algo
las sorprendió
mientras vivían,
en la inmovilidad se desmayaron
y construyeron una ciudad muerta.

Una ciudad sin gritos,
sin cocinas,
un solemne recinto
de pureza,
formas puras caídas
en un desorden sin resurrecciones,
en una multitud que perdió la mirada,
en un gris monasterio condenado
a la verdad desnuda de sus dioses.

THEATER OF THE GODS

It is thus, in the coastlands:
all suddenly caves in, turns contorted,
acerb, impacted,
or static;
heaves up in immutable theaters,
galleries, ships;
or wheels in a circle
of shorn amputations:
the way of the coastland is this:
grapes in the granite,
the moon's rockeries.

Rust stains the stone
orange, green seams
in the lodes of calcareous peace
batter the spray with their keys,
or the rose of the daybreak;
it is thus with the stones:
none can say
if they rise from the sea or return to it,
but the power
that startled the rocks
in the midst of existence
is certain: they fainted into immobility
and left a necropolis there.

A dead city without kitchens
or outcries,
the somber enclave
of their purity,
pure, fallen forms
in a chaos beyond resurrection,
a multitude lost to all vision,
in cells of monastical gray, condemned
to the truth of their godhead laid bare.

EL CAMINANTE

No son tan tristes estas piedras.
Adentro de ellas vive el oro,
tienen semillas de planetas,
tienen campanas en el fondo,
guantes de hierro, matrimonios
del tiempo con las amatistas:
por dentro ríen con rubíes,
se alimentaron de relámpagos.

Por eso, viajero, cuidado
con las tristezas del camino,
con los misterios en los muros.

Me ha costado mucho saber
que no todo vive por fuera
y no todo muere por dentro,
y que la edad escribe letras
con agua y piedra para nadie,
para que nadie sepa dónde,
para que nadie entienda nada.

THE TRAVELER

The stones do not mope.
Within, lives the gold:
the seed-bearing planets
with bells in their depths,
gauntlets of iron, weddings
of time and the amethysts;
within is the laughter of rubies
and the bread of the lightning.

Traveler, beware: keep
a curious eye on the glooms of the highway,
the mysteries crowding the walls.

This I know at great cost:
all life is not outward,
nor is all death from within:
time writes in the ciphers
of water and rock for no one at all,
so that none may envision the sender
and no one be any the wiser.

Cantos Ceremoniales / Ceremonial Songs
1961

Translated by Ben Belitt

FIN DE FIESTA

I

Hoy es el primer día que llueve sobre Marzo,
sobre las golondrinas que bailan en la lluvia,
y otra vez en la mesa está el mar,
todo está como estuvo dispuesto entre las olas,
seguramente así seguirá siendo.

Seguirá siendo, pero yo, invisible,
alguna vez ya no podré volver
con brazos, manos, pies, ojos, entendimiento,
enredados en sombra verdadera.

II

En aquella reunión de tantos invitados
uno por uno fueron regresando a la sombra
y son así las cosas después de las reuniones,
se dispersan palabras, y bocas, y caminos,
pero hacia un solo sitio, hacia no ser, de nuevo
se pusieron a andar todos los separados.

III

Fin de fiesta. . . Llueve sobre Isla Negra,
sobre la soledad tumultuosa, la espuma,
el polo centelleante de la sal derribada,
todo se ha detenido menos la luz del mar.
Y adónde iremos?, dicen las cosas sumergidas.
Qué soy?, pregunta por vez primera el alga,
y una ola, otra ola, otra ola responden:
nace y destruye el ritmo y continúa:
la verdad es amargo movimiento.

IV

Poemas deshabitados, entre cielo y otoño,
sin personas, sin gastos de transporte,
quiero que no haya nadie por un momento en mis versos,
no ver en la arena vacía los signos del hombre,
huellas de pies, papeles muertos, estigmas

PARTY'S END

I

The first rains are here: it is raining today over March
and the swallows that dance in the downpour;
we have the ocean again on our tables,
all is as the wave wills,
and will surely be so again: all

is as it was: but I, one day made invisible,
will relinquish all power of return
in my arms, hands, feet, eyes, my human discernment,
trapped by a shadow's finality.

II

Among the revelers met at the feast,
some move toward the shadows again, this one or that,
as the power that unites us, disposes: later,
words, mouths, and roads go their separate ways,
but the errand is always the same: each presses on
toward the nothingness into which the divided are drawn.

III

Party's end . . . Isla Negra soaks under the rains:
it rains on a tempest of emptiness, on the spray,
on the pole's coruscations exploding in salt;
all ebbs and delays, leaving only a glare on the sea.
Where are we going? asks the drowning redundance of things.
What am I? the seaweed inquires, silent till now,
and is answered in wave after wave after wave:
one rhythm creates and destroys and continues:
truth lies in the bitter mobility.

IV

Those uninhabited poems, between heaven and autumn,
poems without people, transportation expenses:
for a moment, let no living creature enter my verses,
no trace of a man on the sand's empty reaches,
no footprints, dead papers, distinguishing marks

Pablo Neruda / 119

del pasajero, y ahora
estática niebla, color de Marzo, delirio
de aves del mar, petreles, pelícanos, palomas
de la sal, infinito
aire frío,
una vez más antes de meditar y dormir,
antes de usar el tiempo y extenderlo en la noche,
por esta vez la soledad marítima,
boca a boca con el húmedo mes y la agonía
del verano sucio, ver cómo crece el cristal,
cómo sube la piedra a su inexorable silencio,
cómo se derrama el océano sin matar su energía.

V

Nos pasamos la vida preguntando: cuánto?
y vimos a nuestros padres con el cuánto en los ojos,
en la boca, en las manos, cuánto por aquello,
por esto, cuánto por la tierra, por el kilo de pan,
y también por las espléndidas uvas y por los zapatos.
Cuánto cuesta, señor, cuánto cuesta, nos habíamos
vestido de sonrisas aquel día sin duda
y los padres, con ropa remendada, inseguros
entraban al almacén como a una iglesia terrible.
Pero, después, más lejos, fué lo mismo.

VI

No gusta a los estetas la moraleja, murió
cuando la poesía enseñaba al hombre a ser hombre
y además le dejaba un fulgor de violeta en el alma.
Por eso digo dónde y cómo
y en todas partes desde el trono al petróleo
se ensangrentaba el mundo preguntando,
cuánto? y el grano de la cólera crecía
con el cuánto en las sílabas de todos los idiomas,
si digo y sigo seré un violín gastado,
un trovador que agobió la duda y la verdad.

of the traveler—only
the fog's exaltation, the color of March, the sea bird's
delirium, salt petrels, pelicans, pigeons,
the infinite
chill in the air,
shown once, before meditation and dreaming begin,
before time's uses resume, extending themselves in the night,
an ocean of solitude given for only a moment,
mouth pressing mouth in a month of humidity, a soiled
summer's anguish, while I watch how the crystal expands,
how the rock climbs its pitiless silence,
how the ocean destroys itself without marring its energy.

V

We live out our lifetimes asking: How much?
seeing How much? in the eyes of our mothers and fathers,
their mouths and their hands: this and that
for How much? How much for the earth, for a kilo of bread,
for the windfall of grapes, for the shoes on our feet.
How much, mister, how much does it take, slipping
into our smiles for a moment, cocksure,
while our fathers in patches and hand-me-downs, certain
of nothing, entered the warehouses as one enters a terrible temple.
Later, much farther away, nothing has changed.

V I

It displeases the esthete to edify: the poem with a moral
that went out of fashion when the poem taught the man
how to live like a man, leaving behind its violet
cachet in the soul. I speak of the whithers and wherefores
as I choose, from the throne to the oil slick
that bloodies the world, asking
How much? while the grains of my anger grow greater
with my How many? syllables speaking all the world's languages:
yes, I speak, I speak on; and will be, if need be, a cracked violin
or a troubador wracked by the truth and the doubt of the world.

Pablo Neruda / 121

VII

El deber crudo, como es cruda la sangre de una herida
o como es aceptable a pesar de todo el viento frío reciente,
nos hace soldados, nos hace la voz y el paso
de los guerreros, pero es con ternura indecible
que nos llaman la mesa, la silla, la cuchara,
y en plena guerra oímos cómo gritan las copas.
Pero no hay paso atrás! Nosotros escogimos,
nadie pesó en las alas de la balanza
sino nuestra razón abrumadora
y este camino se abrió con nuestra luz:
pasan los hombres sobre lo que hicimos,
y en este pobre orgullo está la vida,
es éste el esplendor organizado.

VIII

Fin de fiesta... Es tiempo de agua,
se mueven los ríos subterráneos de Chile
y horadan el fondo fino de los volcanes,
atraviesan el cuarzo y el oro, acarrean silencio.
Son grandes aguas sagradas que apenas conoce el hombre,
se dice mar, se dice Cabo de Hornos,
pero este reino no tiene mancha humana,
la especie aquí no pudo implantar sus comercios,
sus motores, sus minas, sus banderas,
es libre el agua y se sacude sola,
se mueve y lava, lava,
lava piedras, arenas, utensilios, heridos,
no se consume como el fuego sangriento,
no se convierte en polvo ni en ceniza.

IX

La noche se parece al agua, lava el cielo,
entra en los sueños con un chorro agudo
la noche
tenaz, interrumpida y estrellada,
sola
barriendo los vestigios
de cada día muerto

The brutal imperative, as the blood in a wound may be brutal
or the gathering chill in the wind is made bearable
for all our discomfiture, makes warriors of us, gives us the stance
and inflection of fighters; but still, with unspeakable tenderness,
the table, the spoon, and the chair call out to us:
in the thick of the battle we wait for the cry of the crockery.
But backward is nowhere! Having settled our loyalties,
nothing can lower the balances
but the weight of our reason bearing down on us one way,
and the path we broke open with our common enlightenment:
men move back and forth on our bridge of commitment.
That is the unprepossessing pride of our lifetime,
and its organized splendor.

Party's end . . . . This is the rainy season,
with the underground rivers of Chile on the move
drilling the delicate troughs of volcanoes,
piercing the quartz and the gold, moving the silences.
This is the mighty arcana of water barely known to us here;
though we speak of the sea and name it by name: Cape Horn:
the stain of mortality never mars its dominion,
we can never implant our transactions,
the mines, motors, flags of our species.
Open-ended, the water shakes itself free:
it moves while it cleanses and cleanses:
it cleanses the stone and the sand, our wounds and utensils.
It is never used up, like the bleeding away of the fire,
it does not turn to cinder and ash.

IX

Night and the water are one; it washes the sky,
enters our dreams with the immediate burst of its presence,
night
doggedly there, interrupted and starry,
alone
as it sweeps off the leavings
of every dead day

Pablo Neruda / 123

en lo alto las insignias
de su estirpe nevada
y abajo
entre nosotros
la red de sus cordeles, sueño y sombra.

De agua, de sueño, de verdad desnuda,
de piedra y sombra
somos o seremos,
y los nocturnos no tenemos luz,
bebemos noche pura,
en el reparto nos tocó la piedra
del horno cuando fuimos
a sacar el pan
sacamos sombra
y por la vida
fuimos
divididos:
nos partió la noche,
nos educó en mitades
y anduvimos
sin tregua, traspasados
por estrellas.

X

Los desgranados, los muertos de rostro tierno,
los que amamos, los que brillan
en el firmamento, en la multitud del silencio,
hicieron temblar la espiga con su muerte,
nos pareció morir, nos llevaban con ellos
y quedamos temblando en un hilo, sintiendo la amenaza,
y así siguió la espiga desgranándose
y el ciclo de las vidas continúa.

Pero, de pronto, faltan a la mesa
los más amados muertos, y esperamos,
y no esperamos, es así la muerte,
se va acercando a cada silla y luego
allá ya no se sienta la que amamos,

with the snowy
device of its heraldry over us,
and under us,
between us,
the net with the knots of its cordage: shadow and dream.

Water or dream, truth's nakedness,
shadow and stone—
we are these and continue to be:
our nocturnes say nothing of light,
we drink the pure darkness;
our lot was to stand by the stones
of the oven:
when we bent toward the bread with our paddles
we drew out the darkness
and were broken
into
our lives:
it was night that divided us,
taught us its wisdom by halves
till we walked
without faltering, pierced
by the light of the stars.

                              x
Those threshed out of life, the dead with the delicate faces,
whom we cherished, who burned
in the firmament in a multiple silence
and rippled the wheat with their dying:
the seemingly dead bore off a part of ourselves,
left us poised by a thread, aware of their menace,
while the wheat was flailed finer and finer
and the cycle of living resumed.

All at once, the most preciously dead
are gone from our table. We wait
without ever quite waiting, as one waits for the dead,
while she whom we cherished comes closer,
behind every chair, and will not take her place at the table.

se murió con violín el pobre Alberto,
y se desploma el padre hacia el abuelo.

XI

Construyamos el día que se rompe,
no demos cuerda a cada hora sino
a la importante claridad, al día,
al día que llegó con sus naranjas.
Al fin de cuentas de tantos detalles
no quedará sino un papel
marchito, masticado, que rodará en la arena
y será por inviernos devorado.

Al fin de todo no se recuerda la hoja
del bosque, pero quedan
el olor y el temblor en la memoria:
de aquella selva aún vivo impregnado,
aún susurra en mis venas el follaje,
pero ya no recuerdo día ni hora:
los números, los años son infieles,
los meses se reúnen en un túnel tan largo
que Abril y Octubre suenan como dos piedras locas,
y en un solo canasto se juntan las manzanas,
en una sola red la plata del pescado,
mientras la noche corta con una espada fría
el resplandor de un día que de todas maneras
vuelve mañana, vuelve si volvemos.

XII

Espuma blanca, Marzo en la Isla, veo
trabajar ola y ola, quebrarse la blancura,
desbordar el océano de su insaciable copa,
el cielo estacionario dividido
por largos lentos vuelos de aves sacerdotales
y llega el amarillo,
cambia el color del mes, crece la barba
del otoño marino,
y yo me llamo Pablo,
soy el mismo hasta ahora,

Or unhappy Alberto, dead with his fiddle, there,
the fathers caved in on the grandfathers.

X I

Let us build an expendable day
without winding the hours, counting
only the salient clarity—that day
of all days that came bearing oranges.
The columns close on the niggling particulars,
leaving their chewed scrap of paper
spinning off in the sand,
devoured by the winters.

Not a leaf in the forest
survives our recall, though its scent
and vibration stay in the memory:
in that forest I put forth my foliage
and carry its sigh in my veins
with no thought for the hour or the day.
The years and the numbers betray us:
month follows month in the vast of the tunnel,
October and April clash like two lunatic stones,
the apples rain into one basket,
the silvery catch in one net,
while night with a rapier's precision
cuts through day's splendor—the day
that is ours if we are there to retrieve it tomorrow.

X I I

White spindrift, March on the Island, I see
wave work against wave and splinter the whiteness,
the ungratified cup of the ocean brimming over,
the immovable sky slowly
lengthen and part with the flight of pontifical birds.
We come upon yellow,
the month changes its color, the beard
of the watery autumn grows long:
but my name remains Pablo,
I am just as I was,

Pablo Neruda / 127

tengo amor, tengo dudas,
tengo deudas,
tengo el inmenso mar con empleados
que mueven ola y ola,
tengo tanta intemperie que visito
naciones no nacidas:
voy y vengo del mar y sus países,
conozco
los idiomas de la espina,
el diente del pez duro,
escalofrío de las latitudes,
la sangre del coral, la taciturna
noche de la ballena,
porque de tierra en tierra fui avanzando
estuarios, insufribles territorios,
y siempre regresé, no tuve paz:
qué podía decir sin mis raíces?

XIII

Qué podía decir sin tocar tierra?
A quién me dirigía sin la lluvia?
Por eso nunca estuve donde estuve
y no navegué más que de regreso
y de las catedrales no guardé
retrato ni cabellos: he tratado
de fundar piedra mía a plena mano,
con razón, sin razón, con desvarío,
con furia y equilibrio: a toda hora
toqué los territorios del león
y la torre intranquila de la abeja,
por eso cuando vi lo que ya había visto
y toqué tierra y lodo, piedra y espuma mía,
seres que reconocen mis pasos, mi palabra,
plantas ensortijadas que besaban mi boca,
dije: "aquí estoy," me desnudé en la luz,
dejé caer las manos en el mar,
y cuando todo estaba transparente,
bajo la tierra, me quedé tranquilo.

with my doubts, with my debts,
with my loves,
having a whole sea to myself with its
personnel moving the waves,
pummeled by storms that blow me
toward Cloud-Cuckoo-Land:
I come and I go with the sea and the countries it grazes,
I know
the thorn's languages,
the bite of the obdurate fish,
the chill of the latitudes,
the blood in the coral, the taciturn
night of the whale.
I have pushed past the deltas, from country to country,
the unbearable wastes of the world,
and never found peace. I have always come back.
What can I say without roots?

XIII

What can I say without touching my palms to the land?
To whom shall I turn without rain?
I have never set foot in the countries I lived in,
every port was a port of return:
I have no post cards, no keepsakes of hair
from important cathedrals: I have built what I could
out of natural stone, like a native, open-handed,
I have worked with my reason, unreason, my caprices,
my fury, and poise: hour after hour
I have touched the domains of the lion
and the turbulent tower of the bee:
having seen what there was to be seen,
having handled the clay and the loam, the spray and the rock,
with those who remember my footprints and words,
the tendrils of plants whose kisses remain on my mouth,
I say: "Here is my place," stripping myself down in the light
and dropping my hands in the sea,
until all is transparent again
there under the earth, and my sleep can be tranquil.

III

Yo soy el sumergido de aquellas latitudes,
allí dejé mis manos, mi primera abundancia,
los tesoros vacíos más ricos que el dinero,
el fulgor de aquel mundo de hojas, raíces, sílabas
sin idioma, de hojas entrecortadas
que una a una me hicieron entender una dicha
joven y tenebrosa, y es por eso
que cuando
cayó el humo y el mar, la lava, el miedo
allí cayeron, enredándose en un nudo de espinas
que rodaba temblando sobre el día
con una cola de agua hirsuta y piedras que mordían,
y la tierra paría y moría, agonizaba y nacía,
y otra vez volvía a llamarse tierra y a tener noche
y de nuevo borraba su nombre con espanto,
ay, ay hermanos ausentes, como si el dolor fuera un sistema
    intacto,
una copa de aire amargo entre todo el aire del cielo
allí donde yo estuve llegó a mis labios la muerte,
allí donde yo pasé se sacudió la tierra
y se quemó mi corazón con un solo relámpago.

IV

Cuéntame tú, pobre Pedro, pobre Juan,
tú, pobre, silencioso habitante de las islas,
Agustín Pescador casado con María Selva,
o tú, Martín sin olvido, sin nunca más olvido,
hijo de la memoria pedregosa,
cuéntame, cuéntame sin día ni noche, sin palabras,
solo con lo que perdiste, las redes, el arado,
la casita y el chancho, la máquina Singer comprada en Temuco
a costa de tanto tejido, de tanto trabajo lloviendo,
lloviendo, siempre con la lluvia a cuestas
y los zapatos de toda la familia
que esperan con paciencia el invierno para perforarse y podrirse.
Oh ahora tal vez no significa nada el plazo vencido,

III

I am the underseas man of the latitudes
which have in their keeping my hands, my original plenitude,
the anonymous treasure precious beyond price,
a world dazzling with leaves, roots, syllables
devoid of all language, leaves that still part for the knife, each
bringing me word of a destiny
shadowy, youthful. Thus,
when
the smoke fell, the lava, the seas, the terror
rained down, spun the knots in the shuddering thorn,
circled the days
with a hairy backlash of water and the tooth of the stone,
earth died and brought forth, earth perished and spawned,
called itself earth again, blackened again into night,
blotted its name with its fears
—O my brothers in absence!—as if grief's mandate was
    immutable,
wormwood of air in a cup, in a heaven of air,
it was then I felt death on my lips, in that place,
earth jarred me in passing,
my heart flared in the thunderbolt and grew ashen.

IV

Tell me, poor Peter, poor John,
poor, speechless islander,
Augustine Fisherman wedded to Mary de Forest,
Martin, past man's forgetting, past the turns of forgetfulness,
memory's child in the adamant,
lacking language, daylight and darkness—tell me now
in your language of loss: nets, plows, pigs,
cabins, the Singer Sewing Machine bought in Temuco
at the cost of what crisscrossing threads, what a tempest of labor
under the rain, the back-breaking rains,
while a family's shoes
stolidly braced for a winter to rot and riddle the leather.
No matter now, it may be—the due dates and deadlines,

Pablo Neruda / 131

ni aquel caballo robado que apareció después en Nehuentúe.
Ahora la gran deuda de la vida fué pagada con miedo,
fué volcada en la tierra como una cosecha
de la que todos huían rezando, llorando y muriendo,
sin comprender por qué nacimos, ni por qué la tierra
que esperó tanto tiempo que madurara el trigo
ahora, sin paciencia, como una brusca viuda
borracha y crepitante se hiciera pagar de golpe
amor y amor, vida y vida, muerte y muerte.

v

El cementerio de los Andwanter en la Isla,
frente a Valdivia, escondió cien años
la última gota pura del olvido. Sólo
unos cuantos fundadores muertos, el caballero rubio
y su mujer cocinante, los hijos que devoró el invierno.
Las lianas, las hiedras, las cadenas del bosque,
los hilos que desde el *drimis winterey* y el *notofagus*
altos como las catedrales que perdieron,
góticos como los sueños feroces de su natalicio,
cosieron con aguja y silencio una pequeña patria verde,
la iglesia vegetal que sus huesos quería.
Y ahora, aquellos muertos qué hicieron? Dónde viven?
De aquella taza de agua y olvido, de aquella susurrante
sombra secreta, salió también el miedo
a pasear con su ropa inundada por la soledad de Valdivia?
O también alcanzó allí la lengua del volcán,
el agua interminable que quería matar
y el grito agudo, agudo del mar contra el olvido?

v i

De Puerto Saavedra un patio de amapolas,
el no ser de los indios, la torre del verano
como un faro azotado por las olas del trigo,
duro y azul el cielo de la melancolía,
y una raíz cargada de pólvora y perfume
dentro de mí, naciendo, derribando la luna.

the theft of the horse that turned up in Nehuentúe.
Life is paid back in your staggering debit of fear—
overturned on the earth like a harvest
abandoned by those who dampened it down with their weeping
    and dying
without waiting for answers: why we are born, why earth,
that waits long for a wheat field to ripen, now
turned brutish, irascible, a widow,
drunk, with a plague in her bones, demands her last tittle at once:
a love and a love, a life and a life, a death and a death.

v

The Andwanter's grave plot, facing Valdivia,
a hundred years on the Island, hid
oblivion's last distillation. A bare handful
of founding cadavers: the towheaded gentleman,
his wife with a flair for fine cookery, his sons whom the winter
    devoured.
Liana and ivy, the woods' intrications,
threads spun from the *drimis winterey* and *notofagus,*
vaulted up and were lost like cathedrals,
gothic bad dreams of their barbarous birthday,
stitching with needle and silence, making a green little
fatherland, a vegetable chapel for a devotion of bones.
But what were the dead doing there? Where do they live now?
Could this teacup of water and oblivion, this secretive
rumble of darkness have nurtured the terror
that paces the solitude, with soaked clothes, in Valdivia?
Was it here the volcano licked out its tongue,
the inexhaustible waters intent upon murder,
the outcry thinned to a scream, ocean's cry against all oblivion?

v i

In Puerto Saavedra: a courtyard of poppies,
the nirvana of Indians, the bastion of summer,
a lighthouse assaulted by wave after wave of the wheat,
melancholia's heaven of azure and adamant,
packed with dust and aromas, like a root
driven deep in my being, branching up till it topples the moon.

Pablo Neruda / *133*

El viejo poeta de barba amarilla, pastor del cisne frío,
del cisne errante, cúpula, monarquía de nieve
cápsula clara, nave de los solemnes lagos,
el antiguo poeta que me dió una mano
rápida, fugitiva, antes de irse a su tumba,
ahora qué pudo hacer con su pequeño esqueleto
cuando todo tembló sin cisnes, todo rodó en la lluvia,
y el mar del otro lado devoró el Malecón,
entró por las ventanas odio y agua enemiga,
odio sin fondo, espada de la naturaleza.
Qué pudo hacer mi amigo reducido a semilla,
vuelto a germen, recién tal vez naciendo,
cuando el odio del mar aplastó las maderas
y hasta la soledad quedó sacrificada?

VIII

Adentro está el terror, abajo duerme el terror,
es un óvulo estriado que vive en el fuego,
es una pluma pálida que—máquina o medusa—
sube y baja, recorre las venas del volcán,
hasta que frenética saltó de su recinto
y de larva insondable se transformó en corona,
trueno terrible, tubo total de la tormenta,
rosa de azufre y sangre sobre el dios coronado.
Y aquella paz, aquella nieve en la mentira
del agua quieta, en la paciencia del Llanquihue,
todo aquello, el verano con su paloma inmóvil,
terminó en un silbido de fuego profundo:
se rompió el cielo, galopó la tierra,
y cuando sólo el mar podía responder
se juntaron las aguas en una ola cobarde
que palpitó subiendo por la altura
y cayó con su frío en el infierno.

X

El miedo envuelve los huesos como un nueva piel,
envuelve la sangre con la piel de la noche,
bajo la planta de los pies mueve la tierra:

The old poet, bard of the yellowing beard, herding his swans,
the wandering swans of the cold, cupolas, kingdoms of snow,
chaste capsules, boats on the ceremonial lakes,
the old maker of songs gave me his hand,
furtive and fugitive, before walking off to his grave.
What could he do with the scrap of a skeleton left him
when everything shook with the vanishing swans, all whirled in
   the rain,
and the sea, on the other side of him, demolished the Levee,
the hatred and spite of the waters poured through the windows:
the bottomless rancor, the rapier blade of brute Nature?
What was there left for my friend, now made small as a seedling,
gone back to the grains, born for the first time, it may be,
when ocean's malignity crashed back on the planks
and even its solitude was fed to the flame?

VIII

The terror within, the terror that drowses below,
in the ruts' ovulation, is an egg that lives in the fire,
a feather of pallor—machine or medusa—
that rises and falls, scudding the veins of volcanoes
till it breaks its containment and unfolds in a frenzy,
from the larva's inscrutable changes to the shape of a wreath,
a terrible thunderclap, the encompassing tube of the storm,
roses of sulphur and blood for the crown of a god.
That delusive repose, the snow on a fraudulent
stillness of water, the patience of Llanquihue's
craters, midsummer's motionless dove in the air—all
ends in one syllable of incomprehensible fire:
the whole sky is smashed, earth gallops on
till there is only the sea to give back its answer,
the waters reared up in one cowardly wave
that sways and falls back from its summit
and is hurled freezing again into the fire.

X

Fear bounds the bones of our body, like a graft of new skin,
envelops our blood like a skin that envelops the dark;
under our boot soles, the whole earth is moving.

Pablo Neruda / 135

no es tu pelo, es el miedo en tu cabeza
como una cabellera de clavos verticales
y lo que ves no son las calles rotas
sino, adentro de ti, tus paredes caídas,
tu infinito frustrado, se desploma
otra vez la ciudad, en tu silencio sólo se oye
la amenaza del agua, y en el agua
los caballos ahogados galopan en tu muerte.

XIII

Debajo de mis alas mojadas, hijos, dormid,
amarga población de la noche inestable,
chilenos perdidos en el terror, sin nombre,
sin zapatos, sin padre, ni madre, ni sabiduría:
ahora bajo la lluvia tenderemos
el poncho y a plena muerte, bajo mis alas,
a plena noche dormiremos para despertar:
es nuestro deber eterno la tierra enemiga,
nuestro deber es abrir las manos y los ojos
y salir a contar lo que muere y lo que nace.
No hay infortunio que no reconstruya la aguja
cose que cose el tiempo como una costurera
coser un rosal rojo sobre las cicatrices
y ahora tenemos nuevas islas, volcanes,
nuevos ríos, océano recién nacido,
ahora seamos una vez más: existiremos,
pongámonos en la cara la única sonrisa que flotó sobre el agua,
recojamos el sombrero quemado y el apellido muerto,
vistámonos de nuevo de hombre y de mujer desnudos:
construyamos el muro, la puerta, la ciudad:
comencemos de nuevo el amor y el acero:
fundemos otra vez la patria temblorosa.

Not the separate hairs of your head, but the terrors within it
stand up on end in a fright-wig of vertical nails;
what is shown to your eyes is no longer a crack in the street
but the terrible toppling of walls inside of you,
your thwarted infinity, a city laid waste
again and again; nothing is heard in your silence but
a menace of water, and there in the water-spate,
the drowned horses galloping into your death.

XIII

Under the wet of my wings sleep soundly, my children,
the bitter fraternity of one indeterminate night,
Chile's anonymous children lost in your terror,
fatherless, motherless, shoeless, wanting in cunning:
here under the rain let us spread out our poncho
and in full view of death, under my wings, in
night's total darkness, sleep till we waken again:
the enemy earth is our timeless indenture,
our employment, to open our hands and our eyes,
move out and reckon our losses and gains, our living and dead.
No disaster is proof against the replenishing needle;
however time works in the fabric, a sempstress sewing and sewing,
she will stitch a red rose tree over the cicatrices:
all will be new again: islands, volcanoes,
the river's invention, seas newly shaped out of chaos,
and our selves: let us make ourselves new again, come into
    existence
again, wear on our faces the primordial smile of the water.
Let us reach for our hats in the fire, and our dead appellations,
put on our garment of nakedness again, man and woman,
let us raise up the wall and the door and the city,
begin our loves over again, inaugurate steel:
let us make ready the beams of a tremulous heritage.

LAUTRÉAMONT RECONQUISTADO

I

Cuando llegó a París tuvo mucho que hacer.
Éstas eran las verdaderas calles del hombre.
Aquí las había taladrado como los túneles al gusano
adentro de un queso oscuro, bajo el atroz invierno.
Las casas eran tan grandes que la sabiduría
se empequeñeció y corrió como rata al granero
y sólo fueron habitadas las casas por la sombra,
por la rutina venenosa de los que padecían.
Compró flores, pequeñas flores en el mercado des Halles
y de Clignancourt absorbió el asco militante,
no hubo piedra olvidada para el pequeño Isidoro,
su rostro se fué haciendo delgado como un diente,
delgado y amarillo como la luna menguante en la pampa,
cada vez era más parecido a la luna delgada.
La noche le robaba hora por hora el rostro.
La noche de París ya había devorado
todos los regimientos, las dinastías, los héroes,
los niños y los viejos, las prostitutas, los ricos y los pobres.
Ducasse estaba solo y cuanto tuvo de luz lo entregó cuerpo a
    cuerpo,
contra la devoradora se dispuso a luchar,
fabricó lobos para defender la luz,
acumuló agonía para salvar la vida,
fué más allá del mal para llegar al bien.

II

Lo conocí en el Uruguay cuando era tan pequeño
que se extraviaba en las guitarras del mes de julio,
aquellos días fueron de guerra y de humo,
se desbocaron los ríos, crecieron sin medida las aguas.
No había tiempo para que naciera.
Debió volver muchas veces, remontar el deseo,
viajar hasta su origen, hasta por fin llegar

LAUTRÉAMONT* REGAINED

I

Arriving in Paris, he found there was much to be done.
Here, the streets were authentically human,
drilled through the city like tunnels, or as the worm
works in the dark of the cheese, in winter's barbarity.
The long houses loomed up, as if to belittle
a boast of omniscience that scuttled away like a rat in a granary,
leaving only a shadow,
the poisonous life of routine, to harry the occupants.
He bought a spray of minuscule flowers in the market at Halles,
breathed the militant nausea of Clignancourt;
not a stone went unturned as the little Isidoro
pared his face to the width of a tooth,·
turned sallow and gaunt as the waning moon of the pampas,
took on its diminished equivalence day after day.
Night pillaged his face with each passing hour—
the Parisian night that swallows
whole regiments, heroes and dynasties,
the young and the aged, the haves and have-nots and the whores;
Ducasse was alone, to bear what was left of the light, hand-to-hand
to defy the devourer, fabricate wolves to keep watch on the light,
consolidate anguish and salvage some part of his life—
to thrust past the world's evil in order to come on the good.

II

I knew him in Uruguay—already so tiny
he wandered inside the guitars of July and was lost.
It was a time of warfare and smoke,
when rivers ran rampant, floodwaters swamped all the plummets.
He hardly had time to be born.
Forced backward again and again, climbing every desire,
traveling back to his origins, at last he arrived when

---

* Isidore Ducasse, who later assumed the name of Comte de Lautréamont,
1846–1870, born in Montevideo, Uruguay, educated in the lycées of France,
died in the *faubourg* Montmartre. Author of *Les Chants de Maldoror,* destined
to become a surrealist classic after his death.

cuando sangre y tambores golpeaban a la puerta,
y Montevideo ardía como los ojos del puma.
Turbulenta fué aquella época, y de color morado
como un deshilachado pabellón de asesinos.
Desde la selva el viento militar,
llegaba en un confuso olor a hierba ardiendo.
Los fusiles quebrados a la vera del río
entraban en el agua y a plena medianoche
se habían convertido en guitarras, el viento
repartía sollozos y besos de las barcarolas.

v

Del niño misterioso recojamos
cuanto dejó, sus cantos triturados,
las alas tenebrosas de la nave enlutada,
su negra dirección que ahora entendemos.
Ha sido revelada su palabra.
Detrás de cada sombra suya el trigo.
En cada ojo sin luz una pupila.
La rosa en el espacio del honor.
La esperanza que sube del suplicio.
El amor desbordando de su copa.
El deber hijo puro de la madera.
El rocío que corre saludando a las hojas.
La bondad con más ojos que una estrella.
El honor sin medalla ni castillo.

the blood and the drums were hammering hard at his door
and Montevideo blazed like the eyes of a puma.
Time's turbulence stained the world purple,
an assassin's pavilion in rags.
A bellicose wind from the forests
blew stench and confusion over the blaze of the prairies.
Rifles lay smashed on the river banks;
sank underneath; and at midnight
turned themselves into guitars. The wind
blew its barcaroles, dividing the kisses and tears.

v

From the child we recover the enigmas
he left us: the smashed gift of his songs,
the shadowy wings of the ship of his mourning,
his black destination, known to us now.
His word is revealed.
Behind every shadow, a wheat blade.
In all eyes, an iris to light up the dark.
A rose in the space of his probity.
Hope wafting up from the suppliant.
Love brimming its cup.
Duty's immaculate child in the whorl of the wood.
The dew racing to rally the leaf.
The good, with more eyes than the stars.
Without castles, without medals: his honor.

Plenos Poderes / **Full Powers**
1962

Translated by Alastair Reid

PARA LAVAR A UN NIÑO

Sólo el amor más viejo de la tierra
lava y peina la estatua de los niños,
endereza las piernas, las rodillas,
sube el agua, resbalan los jabones,
y el cuerpo puro sale a respirar
el aire de la flor y de la madre.

Oh vigilancia clara!
Oh dulce alevosía!
Oh tierna guerra!

Ya el pelo era un tortuoso
pelaje entrecruzado por carbones,
por aserrín y aceite,
por hollines, alambres y cangrejos,
hasta que la paciencia
del amor
estableció los cubos, las esponjas,
los peines, las toallas,
y de fregar y de peinar y de ámbar,
de antigua parsimonia y de jazmines
quedó más nuevo el niño todavía
y corrió de las manos de la madre
a montarse de nuevo en su ciclón,
a buscar lodo, aceite, orines, tinta,
a herirse y revolcarse entre las piedras.
Y así recién lavado salta el niño a vivir
porque más tarde sólo tendrá tiempo
para andar limpio, pero ya sin vida.

TO WASH A CHILD

Only the most ancient love on earth
will wash and comb the statue of the children,
straighten the feet and knees.
The water rises, the soap slithers,
and the pure body comes up to breathe
the air of flowers and motherhood.

Oh, the sharp watchfulness,
the sweet deception,
the lukewarm struggle!

Now the hair is a tangled
pelt criscrossed by charcoal,
by sawdust and oil,
soot, wiring, crabs,
until love, in its patience,
sets up buckets and sponges,
combs and towels,
and, out of scrubbing and combing, amber,
primal scrupulousness, jasmines,
has emerged the child, newer still,
running from the mother's arms
to clamber again on its cyclone,
go looking for mud, oil, urine and ink,
hurt itself, roll about on the stones.
Thus, newly washed, the child springs into life,
for, later, it will have time for nothing more
than keeping clean, but with the life lacking.

PÁJARO

Caía de un pájaro a otro
todo lo que el día trae,
iba de flauta en flauta el día,
iba vestido de verdura
con vuelos que abrían un túnel,
y por allí pasaba el viento
por donde las aves abrían
el aire compacto y azul:
por allí entraba la noche.

Cuando volví de tantos viajes
me quedé suspendido y verde
entre el sol y la geografía:
vi cómo trabajan las alas,
cómo se trasmite el perfume
por un telégrafo emplumado
y desde arriba vi el camino,
los manantiales, las tejas,
los pescadores a pescar,
los pantalones de la espuma,
todo desde mi cielo verde.
No tenía más alfabeto
que el viaje de las golondrinas,
el agua pura y pequeñita
del pequeño pájaro ardiendo
que baila saliendo del polen.

BIRD

It fell from one bird to another,
all that the day is bringing.
The day moved from flute to flute,
clothed in vegetation,
its flight forming a tunnel
through which the wind was passing
and birds were breaking open
the close-packed blue air.
That way the night would enter.

When I returned from so many journeys,
I stayed suspended and green
between the sun and geography.
I saw how wings were working,
how perfumes were transmitted
by a feathered telegraph,
and, from above, I saw the path,
the springs and the roof tiles,
the fishermen at their trades,
the trouser-legs of the foam;
I saw it all from my green sky.
I had no more alphabet
than the swallows' migrations,
the tiny, pure sparkle
of the small, fiery bird
which danced out of the pollen.

PLANETA

Hay piedras de agua en la luna?
Hay aguas de oro?
De qué color es el otoño?
Se unen uno a uno los días
hasta que en una cabellera
se desenlazan? Cuánto cae
—papeles, vino, manos, muertos—
de la tierra en esa comarca?

Viven allí los ahogados?

PLANET

Are there stones of water on the moon?
Are there waters of gold?
What color is autumn?
Do the days mesh into each other
until like a shock of hair
they all unravel? How much falls—
paper, wine, hands, dead bodies—
from the earth on that region?

Is that where the drowned live?

ODA PARA PLANCHAR

La poesía es blanca:
sale del agua envuelta en gotas,
se arruga, y se amontona,
hay que extender la piel de este planeta,
hay que planchar el mar de su blancura
y van y van las manos,
se alisan las sagradas superficies
y así se hacen las cosas:
las manos hacen cada día el mundo,
se une el fuego al acero,
llegan el lino, el lienzo y el tocuyo
del combate de las lavanderías
y nace de la luz una paloma:
la castidad regresa de la espuma.

IN PRAISE OF IRONING

Poetry is pure white:
it emerges from the water covered with drops,
all wrinkled, in a heap.
It has to be spread out, the skin of this planet,
has to be ironed, the sea in its whiteness;
and the hands keep on moving,
smoothing the holy surfaces.
So are things accomplished.
Each day, hands re-create the world,
fire is married to steel,
and the canvas, the linens and the cottons return
from the skirmishing of the laundries;
and out of light is born a dove.
Out of the froth once more comes chastity.

A LA TRISTEZA

Tristeza, necesito
tu ala negra,
tanto sol, tanta miel en el topacio
cada rayo sonríe
en la pradera
y todo es luz redonda en torno mío,
todo es abeja eléctrica en la altura.
Por eso
tu ala negra
dame,
hermana tristeza:
necesito que alguna vez se apague
el zafiro y que caiga
la oblicua enredadera de la lluvia,
el llanto de la tierra:
quiero
aquel madero roto en el estuario,
la vasta casa a oscuras
y mi madre
buscando
parafina
y llenando la lámpara
hasta no dar la luz sino un suspiro.

La noche no nacía.

El día resbalaba
hacia su cementerio provinciano,
y entre el pan y la sombra
me recuerdo
a mí mismo
en la ventana
mirando lo que no era,
lo que no sucedía
y un ala negra de agua que llegaba
sobre aquel corazón que allí tal vez
olvidé para siempre, en la ventana.

TO SORROW

Sorrow, I need
your black wing.
So much sun, so much honey in the topaz,
each ray smiling
in the meadow
and all is abundant light about me,
all like a whirring bee in the high air.
And so
give me
your black wing,
sister sorrow,
I need sometimes the sapphire to be
extinguished, and the oblique
mesh of the rain to fall,
the weeping of the earth;
I long for
that battered hulk in the estuary,
the great house in darkness
and my mother
searching
for paraffin
and filling the lamp,
never bringing light to birth without a sigh.

Night did not come to birth.

The day was slipping away
toward its own local cemetery,
and, between bread and shade,
I have a memory
of myself
in the window,
looking at what was not,
at what was not happening
and a black wing of water coming down
over that heart which there perhaps
I forgot forever, there in the window.

Pablo Neruda / 153

Ahora echo de menos
la luz negra.

Dame tu lenta sangre,
lluvia
fría,
dame tu vuelo atónito!
A mi pecho
devuélvele la llave
de la puerta cerrada,
destruida.
Por un minuto, por
una corta vida,
quítame luz y déjame
sentirme
perdido y miserable,
temblando entre los hilos
del crepúsculo,
recibiendo en el alma
las manos
temblorosas
de
la
lluvia.

Now I am missing
the black light.

Give me your slow blood,
cold
rain,
give me your fearful spread!
Give back into my keeping
the key
of the closed door,
ruined.
For a minute, for
a short life,
take away my light and leave me
to realize
my misery, my alienation,
trembling in the web
of twilight,
receiving into my being
the trembling
hands
of
the
rain.

A "LA SEBASTIANA"

Yo construí la casa.

La hice primero de aire.
Luego subí en el aire la bandera
y la dejé colgada
del firmamento, de la estrella, de
la claridad y de la oscuridad.

Cemento, hierro, vidrio,
eran la fábula,
valían más que el trigo y como el oro,
había que buscar y que vender,
y así llegó un camión:
bajaron sacos
y más sacos,
la torre se agarró a la tierra dura
—pero, no basta, dijo el Constructor,
falta cemento, vidrio, fierro, puertas—,
y no dormí en la noche.

Pero crecía,
crecían las ventanas
y con poco,
con pegarle al papel y trabajar
y arremeterle con rodilla y hombro
iba a crecer hasta llegar a ser,
hasta poder mirar por la ventana,
y parecía que con tanto saco
pudiera tener techo y subiría
y se agarrara, al fin, de la bandera
que aún colgaba del cielo sus colores.

Me dediqué a las puertas más baratas,
a las que habían muerto

TO "LA SEBASTIANA"*

I built the house.

I built it first in air.
Afterward, in the air, I raised the flag,
and left it draped
from the firmament, from a star, from
clear light and darkness.

Cement, iron and glass
made up the tale.
They were worth more than grain, and, as with gold,
it was necessary to go looking and to sell,
and so a truck arrived.
They unloaded sacks
and more sacks.
The tower took grip in the hard ground—
but not enough, the Builder said;
it needs cement, glass, iron, doors—
and I did not sleep all night.

But it kept growing.
The windows grew,
and with a little more,
sticking to the desk, working,
digging in with knee and shoulder,
it kept on growing to the point of coming to be,
to the point of being able to look through the window,
and it seemed that, after such a welter of sacks,
a roof would rise, which would go up and finally
get a hand on the flag
which was still festooning the sky with its colors.

I applied myself to doors, to the less expensive ones,
those which had finally died,

---

* Neruda's house in Valparaíso. Built over a movie theater and recently
destroyed in a hurricane.

y habían sido echadas de sus casas,
puertas sin muro, rotas,
amontonadas en demoliciones,
puertas ya sin memoria,
sin recuerdo de llave,
y yo dije: "Venid
a mí, puertas perdidas:
os daré casa y muro
y mano que golpea,
oscilaréis de nuevo abriendo el alma,
custodiaréis el sueño de Matilde
con vuestras alas que volaron tanto."

Entonces la pintura
llegó también lamiendo las paredes,
las vistió de celeste y de rosado
para que se pusieran a bailar.
Así la torre baila,
cantan las escaleras y las puertas,
sube la casa hasta tocar el mástil,
pero falta dinero:
faltan clavos,
faltan aldabas, cerraduras, mármol.
Sin embargo, la casa
sigue subiendo
y algo pasa, un latido
circula en sus arterias:
es tal vez un serrucho que navega
como un pez en el agua de los sueños
o un martillo que pica
como alevoso cóndor carpintero
las tablas del pinar que pisaremos.

Algo pasa y la vida continúa.

La casa crece y habla,
se sostiene en sus pies,
tiene ropa colgada en un andamio,
y como por el mar la Primavera

and were consequently pitched out of their houses—
doors without walls, broken,
piled up on demolition sites,
doors by now without memories,
no memory of a key;
and I said: "Come
to me, you abandoned doors.
I shall give you a house and a wall
and a fist to knock on you.
You will swing to and fro once more at the soul's emerging,
you will guard Matilda's sleep
with your wings, that have fluttered so much."

Then came the paint too,
licking the walls.
I dressed them in sky-blue and pink
so that they would begin to dance.
So does the tower dance,
the doors and staircases sing,
the house stretch up to touch its crown—
but money is short,
nails are short,
door knockers, locks and marble.
Nevertheless, the house
continues to rise up, a continuing
throb in its arteries.
Perhaps it is a saw, seething
like a fish in the waters of all dreams,
or a hammer which taps
like a sleazy condor-carpenter
at the boards of pinewood we will be walking on.

Some things go past and living goes on.

The house grows and speaks,
stands on its own feet,
has clothing wrapped around its skeleton,
and, as from the sea the spring,

Pablo Neruda / 159

nadando como náyade marina
besa la arena de Valparaíso,

ya no pensemos más: ésta es la casa:

ya todo lo que falta será azul,

lo que ya necesita es florecer.

Y eso es trabajo de la primavera.

swimming like a naiad of the waters,
kisses the sand beach of Valparaíso,

let us not think any more. This is the house:

from now on, all the things we need will be blue,

what it needs now is a spell of blooming.

And that is the kind of work for spring.

LA PRIMAVERA

El pájaro ha venido
a dar la luz:
de cada trino suyo
nace el agua.

Y entre agua y luz que el aire desarrollan
ya está la primavera inaugurada,
ya sabe la semilla que ha crecido,
la raíz se retrata en la corola,
se abren por fin los párpados del polen.

Todo lo hizo un pájaro sencillo
desde una rama verde.

SPRING

The bird has arrived
to give light.
From every trill of his,
water is born.

And between water and light which unwind the air,
now is the spring inaugurated,
now the seed is aware that it has grown;
the root is posing in the corolla,
at last the eyelids of the pollen lift.

All this accomplished by a simple bird
from his perch on a green bough.

SUMARIO

Estoy contento con tantos deberes
que me impuse, en mi vida
se amasaron extraños materiales:
tiernos fantasmas que me despeinaban,
categóricas manos minerales,
un viento sin razón que me agitaba,
la espina de unos besos lacerantes, la dura realidad
de mis hermanos,
mi deber imperioso de vigía,
mi inclinación a ser sólo yo mismo
en la debilidad de mis placeres,
por eso—agua en la piedra—fué mi vida
cantando entre la dicha y la dureza.

SUMMARY

I am happy with the mountainous debts
I took on myself. In my life,
a welter of odd material things have accumulated—
feeble ghosts which went on upsetting me,
insistent material manipulations,
an inexplicable wind which ruffled me,
the stab of some wounding kisses, the hard reality
of my brothers,
the rigid demand on myself of watchfulness,
the impulse to stay myself, myself alone,
in a weakness of self-pleasuring.
For that reason—water on stone—my life has been
a singing between the chance and the requirement.

PARA TODOS

De pronto no puedo decirte
lo que yo te debo decir,
hombre, perdóname, sabrás
que aunque no escuches mis palabras
no me eché a llorar ni a dormir
y que contigo estoy sin verte
desde hace tiempo y hasta el fin.

Yo comprendo que muchos piensen,
y qué hace Pablo? Estoy aquí.
Si me buscas en esta calle
me encontrarás con mi violín
preparado para cantar
y para morir.

No es cuestión a nadie,
ni menos a aquéllos, ni a ti,
y si escuchas bien, en la lluvia,
podrás oír
que vuelvo y voy y me detengo.
Y sabes que debo partir.

Si no se saben mis palabras
no dudes que soy el que fuí.
No hay silencio que no termine.
Cuando llegue el momento, espérame,
y que sepan todos que llego
a la calle, con mi violín.

FOR EVERYONE

I cannot tell you at once
what I ought to be telling you.
Friend, forgive me; you'll know
that although you don't hear my words,
I neither wept nor went to sleep,
that without seeing you I'm with you
for a long time now, and until the end.

I know that many are thinking,
What is Pablo doing? I am here.
If you look for me in this street,
you will find me, with my violin,
prepared to break into song,
prepared to die.

It is not a question of abandoning anyone,
much less those ones, or you,
and, if you listen well in the rain,
you will be able to hear
that I return, or leave, or linger.
And you realize I must leave.

If my words are not aware of it,
do not doubt, I am he who left.
There is no silence which does not end.
When the moment comes, wait for me,
and let them all know I am arriving
in the street with my violin.

PLENOS PODERES

A puro sol escribo, a plena calle,
a pleno mar, en donde puedo canto,
sólo la noche errante me detiene
pero en su interrupción recojo espacio,
recojo sombra para mucho tiempo.

El trigo negro de la noche crece
mientras mis ojos miden la pradera
y así de sol a sol hago las llaves:
busco en la oscuridad las cerraduras
y voy abriendo al mar las puertas rotas
hasta llenar armarios con espuma.

Y no me canso de ir y de volver,
no me para la muerte con su piedra,
no me canso de ser y de no ser.

A veces me pregunto si de donde
si de padre o de madre o cordillera
heredé los deberes minerales,

los hilos de un océano encendido
y sé que sigo y sigo porque sigo
y canto porque canto y porque canto.

No tiene explicación lo que acontece
cuando cierro los ojos y circulo
como entre dos canales submarinos,
uno a morir me lleva en su ramaje
y el otro canta para que yo cante.

Así pues de no ser estoy compuesto
y como el mar asalta el arrecife
con cápsulas saladas de blancura
y retrata la piedra con la ola,
así lo que en la muerte me rodea
abre en mí la ventana de la vida
y en pleno paroxismo estoy durmiendo.
A plena luz camino por la sombra.

FULL POWERS

I write in the clear sun, in the teeming street,
at full sea-tide, in a place where I can sing;
only the wayward night inhibits me,
but, interrupted by it, I recover space,
I gather shadows to last me a long time.

The black crop of the night is growing
while my eyes meanwhile take measure of the meadows.
So, from one sun to the next, I forge the keys.
In the darkness, I look for the locks
and keep on opening broken doors to the sea,
for it to fill the wardrobes with its foam.

And I do not weary of going and returning.
Death, in its stone aspect, does not halt me.
I am weary neither of being nor of non-being.

Sometimes I puzzle over origins—
was it from my father, my mother or the mountains
that I inherited debts to minerality,

the fine threads spreading from a sea on fire?
And I know that I keep on going for the going's sake,
and I sing because I sing and because I sing.

There is no way of explaining what does happen
when I close my eyes and waver
as between two lost channels under water.
One lifts me in its branches toward my dying,
and the other sings in order that I may sing.

And so I am made up of a non-being,
and, as the sea goes battering at a reef
in wave on wave of salty white-tops
and drags back stones in its retreating wash,
so what there is in death surrounding me
opens in me a window out to living,
and, in the spasm of being, I go on sleeping.
In the full light of day, I walk in the shade.

Pablo Neruda / *169*

Memorial de Isla Negra / Black Island Memorial
1964

Translated by Ben Belitt

I: Dónde nace la lluvia

NACIMIENTO

Nació un hombre
entre muchos
que nacieron,
viví entre muchos hombres
que vivieron,
y esto no tiene historia
sino tierra,
tierra central de Chile, donde
las viñas encresparon sus cabelleras verdes,
la uva se alimenta de la luz,
el vino nace de los pies del pueblo.

Parral se llama el sitio
del que nació
en invierno.

Ya no existen
la casa ni la calle:
soltó la cordillera
sus caballos,
se acumuló
el profundo
poderío,
brincaron las montañas
y cayó el pueblo
envuelto
en terremoto.
Y así muros de adobe,
retratos en los muros,
muebles desvencijados
en las salas oscuras,
silencio entrecortado por las moscas,
todo volvió
a ser polvo:

I: Where the Rain Begins

BIRTH

A man born
among
multitudes,
I lived among multitudes
living—
no matter for history:
it is land,
the heartland of Chile that matters, where
green hair grows dense in the vineyards,
the grape lives on light
and under the feet of a people, wine is born.

Parral is the name
for
what winter brought forth.

The house and the street
no longer stand.
The mountain untethered
its horses,
power
massed
in the depths,
the ranges kicked
upward
and a village fell
gutted
by earthquake.
The mud walls, the portraits nailed to the walls,
the tatterdemalion furniture
in shadowy parlors,
the silence crosscut by the flies,
sank back
into dust: we are

sólo algunos guardamos
forma y sangre,
sólo algunos, y el vino.

Siguió el vino viviendo
subiendo hasta las uvas
desgranadas
por el otoño
errante,
bajó a lagares sordos,
a barricas
que se tiñeron con su suave sangre,
y allí bajo el espanto
de la tierra terrible
siguió desnudo y vivo.

Yo no tengo memoria
del paisaje ni tiempo,
ni rostros, ni figuras,
sólo polvo impalpable,
la cola del verano
y el cementerio en donde
me llevaron
a ver entre las tumbas
el sueño de mi madre.
Y como nunca vi
su cara
la llamé entre los muertos, para verla,
pero como los otros enterrados,
no sabe, no oye, no contestó nada,
y allí se quedó sola, sin su hijo,
huraña y evasiva
entre las sombras.
Y de allí soy, de aquel
Parral de tierra temblorosa,
tierra cargada de uvas
que nacieron
desde mi madre muerta.

only a handful keeping
semblance and kinship together,
a mere handful, and the wine.

The wine went on living:
it climbed up the
grapes
that a vagabond
autumn had scattered,
it sank in the wine presses,
loading the hogsheads
and staining them smooth with its blood; alive
in its dread
of that terrible earth,
naked and vital, it thrived.

I remember nothing
of weather or countryside,
faces or figures—just dust,
impalpable dust,
a tag end of summer,
a graveyard
where once I was brought
to search in the gravestones
for the sleep of my mother.
Her face
was unknown to me,
so I called to her, hoping to summon her face from the dead;
but she stayed with the buried ones,
she knew nothing, heard nothing, answered nothing at all,
keeping her distance, apart from her son,
elusive and shy
in the dark.
That's where I come from:
a quake-ridden soil, from Parral,
a land loaded with grapes
springing up
from the death of my mother.

EL PADRE

El padre brusco vuelve
de sus trenes:
reconocimos
en la noche
el pito
de la locomotora
perforando la lluvia
con un aullido errante,
un lamento nocturno,
y luego
la puerta que temblaba;
el viento en una ráfaga
entraba con mi padre
y entre las dos pisadas y presiones
la casa
se sacudía,
las puertas asustadas
se golpeaban con seco
disparo de pistolas,
las escalas gemían
y una alta voz
recriminaba, hostil,
mientras la tempestuosa
sombra, la lluvia como catarata
despeñada en los techos
ahogaba poco a poco
el mundo
y no se oía nada más que el viento
peleando con la lluvia.

Sin embargo, era diurno.
Capitán de su tren, del alba fría,
y apenas despuntaba
el vago sol, allí estaba su barba,
sus banderas
verdes y rojas, listos los faroles,
el carbón de la máquina en su infierno,

FATHER

The brusque father comes back
from his trains:
we could pick out
his train whistle
cutting the rain,
a locomotive's
nocturnal lament
an unplaceable howl
in the dark.
Later,
the door started trembling.
Wind entered
in gusts with my father;
and between the two advents, footfalls and tensions,
the house
staggered,
a panic of doorways
exploded with a dry
sound of pistols,
stairs groaned
and a shrill voice
nagged hatefully on
in the turbulent
dark. Rain
flooded the roof tops,
the world drowned
by degrees, there
was only the wind's sound
trading blows with the rain.

Still, he was punctual.
Commanding his train in the freeze of the morning,
the sun barely
aloft in the sky, he was there with his beard
and his green and red
signal flags, lanterns ready,
the engine-coal blazing like hellfire,

la Estación con los trenes en la bruma
y su deber hacia la geografía.

El ferroviario es marinero en tierra
y en los pequeños puertos sin marina
—pueblos del bosque—el tren corre que corre
desenfrenando la naturaleza,
cumpliendo su navegación terrestre.
Cuando descansa el largo tren
se juntan los amigos,
entran, se abren las puertas de mi infancia,
la mesa se sacude,
al golpe de una mano ferroviaria
chocan los gruesos vasos del hermano
y destella
el fulgor
de los ojos del vino.

Mi pobre padre duro
allí estaba, en el eje de la vida,
la viril amistad, la copa llena.
Su vida fué una rápida milicia
y entre su madrugar y sus caminos,
entre llegar para salir corriendo,
un día con más lluvia que otros días
el conductor José del Carmen Reyes
subió al tren de la muerte y hasta ahora no ha vuelto.

the Station House showing coach after coach through the fog—
to settle his debt with geography.

Railroader, land-sailor
touching ports with no seacoasts
—whistle stops in the woods—the train races on
brakeless as nature
in its terrestrial voyage.
Not till it rests all
its length on the rails and friends greet
and come in, do the doors of my infancy open:
the table is shaken again
by a railroader's fist
knocking thick glass together, a brotherhood
glowing,
flashing sparks
from the eyes in the wine.

Poor, durable father,
there on the axle of life,
virile in friendships, your cup overflowing:
the whole of your life was a headlong militia;
between daybreaks and roadbeds,
comings and goings, you lived on the double.
Then, on the rainiest day of them all,
the conductor, José del Carmen Reyes,
boarded his death train and has not come back to us since.

LA CONDICIÓN HUMANA

Detrás de mí hacia el Sur, el mar había
roto los territorios con su glacial martillo,
desde la soledad arañada el silencio
se convirtió de pronto en archipiélago,
y verdes islas fueron ciñendo la cintura
de mi patria
como polen o pétalos de una rosa marina
y, aún más, eran profundos los bosques encendidos
por luciérnagas, el lodo era fosforescente,
dejaban caer los árboles largos cordeles secos
como en un circo, y la luz iba de gota en gota
como la bailarina verde de la espesura.

Yo crecí estimulado por razas silenciosas,
por penetrantes hachas de fulgor maderero,
por fragancias secretas de tierra, ubres y vino:
mi alma fué una bodega perdida entre los trenes
en donde se olvidaron durmientes y barricas,
alambre, avena, trigo, cochayuyo, tablones,
y el invierno con sus negras mercaderías.

Así mi cuerpo fué extendiéndose, de noche
mis brazos eran nieve,
mis pies el territorio huracanado,
y crecí como un río al aguacero,
y fuí fértil con todo
lo que caía en mí, germinaciones,
cantos entre hoja y hoja, escarabajos
que procreaban, nuevas
raíces que ascendieron
al rocío,
tormentas que aún sacuden
las torres del laurel, el racimo escarlata
del avellano, la paciencia
sagrada del alerce,
y así mi adolescencia
fué territorio, tuve
islas, silencio, monte, crecimiento,
luz volcánica, barro de caminos,
humo salvaje de palos quemados.

THE HUMAN CONDITION

Southward behind me, an ocean had
broken the mainland with its glacial hammer;
suddenly silence reared archipelagos
in the spidery solitude,
green islands circled the waist
of my country
like pollen or petals, the rose of old ocean,
as ever more deeply the timberland kindled
with fireflies, the mud shone like phosphorus,
trees lowered their parched lengths of cordage like
circuses, light traveled, drop into drop,
a green ballerina of density.

I was nurtured by taciturn races,
the ax's slash in the fullness of timber,
earth's secretive fragrances, udders and wines:
my soul was a market place lost among trains,
where crossties and hogsheads, wire cable, wheat,
cochayuyo, cut planks, lay forgotten
with a winter's somber commodities.

My body extended itself, my arms
turned to snow in the night,
my feet into hurricane country;
I rose like a river under the gush of the rain,
fertile with all that moved into me, germinations,
songs rising leaf over leaf, the mating
of beetles, young
roots thrusting up
in the dew,
deluges shaking
the towers of the laurel, the hazelnut's
clustering scarlet and the holy
forbearance of larches:
my whole adolescence
was dominion,
islands, silence, gestations, and mountains,
the volcanical light and the mud of the road
and smoke rising raw on scorched timber.

EL NIÑO PERDIDO

Lenta infancia de donde
como de un pasto largo
crece el duro pistilo,
la madera del hombre.

Quién fuí? Qué fuí? Qué fuimos?

No hay respuesta. Pasamos.
No fuimos. Éramos. Otros pies,
otras manos, otros ojos.
Todo se fué mudando hoja por hoja
en el árbol. Y en ti? Cambió tu piel,
tu pelo, tu memoria. Aquel no fuiste.
Aquel fué un niño que pasó corriendo
detrás de un río, de una bicicleta,
y con el movimiento
se fué tu vida con aquel minuto.
La falsa identidad siguió tus pasos.
Día a Día las horas se amarraron,
pero tú ya no fuiste, vino el otro,
el otro tú, y el otro hasta que fuiste,
hasta que te sacaste
del propio pasajero,
del tren, de los vagones de la vida,
de la substitución, del caminante.

La máscara del niño fué cambiando,
adelgazó su condición doliente,
aquietó su cambiante poderío:
el esqueleto se mantuvo firme,
la construcción del hueso se mantuvo,
la sonrisa,
el paso, un gesto volador, el eco
de aquel niño desnudo
que salió de un relámpago,
pero fué el crecimiento como un traje!
era otro el hombre y lo llevó prestado.

LITTLE BOY LOST

Slow childhood, a long
pasture for grazing, out of which
grows the hard pistil,
the fiber and wood of the man.

But who was I? What? What were we both?

Nothing answers me now: let it pass.
Being never was once: we went on being. Other feet,
other hands, other eyes.
All things in their passing kept changing, like leaf after leaf
on a tree. And in you? Your skin changed,
your hair and your memory: you were never that other.
That was a child loping by at a run,
a boy on a bicycle on the opposite side of the river,
in whose motion
your whole life passed by in the stress of a moment.
The fraud of identity followed your footsteps.
Day in, day out, hours joined in their sequences,
but none of them held you forever; it was that other
who came, that other you, biding his time till you went,
till you parted yourself
from that intimate sojourner,
from the wagons and trains of your life,
substitutions and wayfarers.

The child's mask kept changing,
his mournful occasions subsided,
he steadied his altering mastery:
his skeleton toughened,
the device of his bones was accomplished,
his smile,
his manner of walking, the fugitive gesture that echoed
the child running nakedly
under a lightning flash—
all that growth was cloth for a garment:
haberdashery loaned to that other!

Pablo Neruda / 183

Así pasó conmigo.

De silvestre
llegué a ciudad, a gas, a rostros crueles
que midieron mi luz y mi estatura,
llegué a mujeres que en mí se buscaron
como si a mí se me hubieran perdido,
y así fué sucediendo
el hombre impuro,
hijo del hijo puro,
hasta que nada fué como había sido,
y de repente apareció en mi rostro
un rostro de extranjero
y era también yo mismo:
era yo que crecía,
eras tú que crecías,
era todo,
y cambiamos
y nunca más supimos quiénes éramos,
y a veces recordamos
al que vivió en nosotros
y le pedimos algo, tal vez que nos recuerde,
que sepa por lo menos que fuimos él, que hablamos
con su lengua,
pero desde las horas consumidas
aquél nos mira y no nos reconoce.

Yes, it was that way.

From a wilderness world
I came to the city: into gasses, into barbarous
faces that measured my light to my stature;
women who sought part of themselves in myself
as though they were lost to me there—
all kept on happening,
one man impurely persisting,
son of the purely born son,
till nothing remained as it was.
Little by little, the face of a stranger
looked out of my face—
though my face remained changelessly there.
It was I who was growing there,
I and yourself,
it was you growing there,
all of us one,
all growing and changing
till no one could say who we were.
Sometimes we remember
the presence that lived with us,
there is something we want from him—that he remember us,
    maybe,
or know, at least, we were he and now talk
with his tongue;
but there in the wreckage of hours
he looks at us, acknowledging nothing.

Lago Budi, sombrío, pesada piedra oscura,
agua entre grandes bosques insepulta,
allí te abrías como puerta subterránea
cerca del solitario mar del fin del mundo.
Galopábamos por la infinita arena
junto a las millonarias espumas derramadas,
ni una casa, ni un hombre, ni un caballo,
sólo el tiempo pasaba y aquella orilla verde
y blanca, aquel océano.
Luego hacia las colinas y, de pronto,
el lago, el agua dura y escondida,
compacta luz, alhaja del anillo terrestre.
Un vuelo blanco y negro: los cisnes ahuyentaron
largos cuellos nocturnos, patas de cuero rojo,
y la nieve serena volando sobre el mundo.

Oh vuelo desde el agua equivalente,
mil cuerpos destinados a la inmóvil belleza
como la transparente permanencia del lago.
De pronto todo fué carrera sobre el agua,
movimiento, sonido, torres de luna llena,
y luego alas salvajes que desde el torbellino
se hicieron orden, vuelo, magnitud sacudida,
y luego ausencia, un temblor blanco en el vacío.

SWAN LAKE

Lake Budi, lackluster, the dark, weighted stone,
forest on forest, with unburied water between:
you opened for me like an underground door
near the sea's solitude, at the world's end.
We galloped the infinite sand
by the seaspray, the millionaire crashing of foam:
not a house, not a man or a horse—nothing
but time passing, the green-and-white
line of the sea-sand, the ocean.
We beat toward the hills; and all at once
the hard, hidden water was there, the lake
compact in a dazzle, the terrestrial ring with its jewel.
A black-and-white panic in air, the swans going up
on feet of red leather, their stretched necks nocturnal,
a halcyon snow soaring over the whole of a world.

O flight from the water's equivalence,
a thousand bodies in air, intent on the beautiful,
fixed like the lake in its orbit, transparent, unchangeable!
Till suddenly all hurtled forward, was uproar, unrest,
a melee on the waters, the towering full of the moon;
then barbarous wings in the whirlwind
turning all into order, tremulous magnitude, flying;
last of all, silence: a white perturbation of vacancy.

II: La luna en el laberinto

EL OPIO EN EL ESTE

Ya desde Singapore olía a opio.
El buen inglés sabía lo que hacía.
En Ginebra tronaba
contra los mercaderes clandestinos
y en las Colonias cada puerto
echaba un tufo de humo autorizado
con número oficial y licencia jugosa.
El gentleman oficial de Londres
vestido de impecable ruiseñor
(con pantalón rayado y almidón de armadura)
trinaba contra el vendedor de sombras,
pero aquí en el oriente
se desenmascaraba
y vendía el letargo en cada esquina.

Quise saber. Entré. Cada tarima
tenía su yacente,
nadie hablaba, nadie reía, creí
que fumaban en silencio.
Pero chasqueaba junto a mí la pipa
al cruzarse la llama con la aguja
y en esa aspiración de la tibieza
con el humo lechoso entraba al hombre
una estática dicha, alguna puerta lejos
se abría hacia un vacío suculento:
era el opio la flor de la pereza,
el goce inmóvil,
la pura actividad sin movimiento.

Todo era puro o parecía puro,
todo en aceite y gozne resbalaba
hasta llegar a ser sólo existencia,
no ardía nada, ni lloraba nadie,
no había espacio para los tormentos
y no había carbón para la cólera.

II: The Moon in the Labyrinth

OPIUM IN THE EAST

From Singapore on, all smelled of opium.
The good folk of England know how to manage.
In Geneva they ranted
about an underground market in drugs
while every Colonial port smoked
in a pillar of authorized opium
stamped with a government number and a juicy entitlement.
The legitimate gentleman from London
impeccably dressed like a nightingale
(pin stripes on his cutaway, starched like an armament)
trilled about "shadow-merchants,"
but here in the East
he showed his true colors
and peddled his lethargies on every street corner.

I wanted to know. I went in. There were the ledges
with the addicts laid out,
nobody spoke, nobody laughed, all seemed
to be smoking in silence.
Then a pipe next to me crackled
as the needle point crossed with the flame:
a tepid well-being rose
with the milky effluvium, and the wraith
of his ecstasy blissfully entered the man, some faraway door
opened up on a succulent void:
the flower of the opium's sloth,
the immobilized joy
of pure act transcending all motion.

All turned to purity, or seemed to be made pure,
all slithered on hinges and oils
till the quick of existence was touched
and nothing was left for the flame, nobody mourned,
there was no room for agony,
no coal for the wrath of the world.

Pablo Neruda / *189*

Miré: pobres caídos,
peones, coolies de ricksha o plantación,
desmedrados trotantes,
perros de calle,
pobres maltratados.
Aquí, después de heridos,
después de ser no seres sino pies,
después de no ser hombres sino brutos de carga,
después de andar y andar y sudar y sudar
y sudar sangre y ya no tener alma,
aquí estaban ahora,
solitarios,
tendidos,
los yacentes por fin, los pata dura:
cada uno con hambre había comprado
un oscuro derecho a la delicia,
y bajo la corola del letargo,
sueño o mentira, dicha o muerte, estaban
por fin en el reposo que busca toda vida,
respetados, por fin, en una estrella.

I saw them: poor, fallen creatures, all,
peons and coolies delivered from rickshaws and plantations,
trotters trodden to pieces,
street mongrels,
the injured and indigent.
Here, after bloodlettings,
after leg work devoid of all living, brute
beasts of burden
plodding and plodding and sweating and sweating,
sweating blood, deprived of their souls—
it was here they all came, in the end.
Prostrate
and alone,
stretched out to the length of their hard little hooves,
each came with his hunger and the price
to buy into the sweets of a shady prerogative—
all gathered under a torpor's corolla,
dream or delusion, good luck or disaster—this was
the peace that eluded their lifetime, at last, their
place in the world, under a star, in the end.

RELIGIÓN EN EL ESTE

Allí en Rangoon comprendí que los dioses
eran tan enemigos como Dios
del pobre ser humano.
                                    Dioses
de alabastro tendidos
como ballenas blancas,
dioses dorados como las espigas,
dioses serpientes enroscados
al crimen de nacer,
budhas desnudos y elegantes
sonriendo en el coktail
de la vacía eternidad
como Cristo en su cruz horrible,
todos dispuestos a todo,
a imponernos su cielo,
todos con llagas o pistola
para comprar piedad o quemarnos la sangre,
dioses feroces del hombre
para esconder la cobardía,
y allí todo era así,
toda la tierra olía a cielo,
a mercadería celeste.

RELIGION IN THE EAST

It came to me there in Rangoon—all gods
are our enemies, like the God
of our humbled humanity.
                         The gods
of the worked alabaster,
poised like white whales;
gods gilded like sheaves
or wreathed in the crime
of conception, like serpents;
the finical nudes of the Buddha
smiling into his cocktail
of eternal vacuity
like Christ on his odious cross—
each stopping at nothing, taking
the kingdom of heaven by force,
ready with pistol and ulcer
to purchase our piety or burn in the blood:
the implacable gods of the human
who conceal every cowardice.
It cames to me there in Rangoon,
till the whole earth stank of heaven
and the heavenly junk turned to chattel.

From AMORES

Terusa 1.

Terusa
abierta entre las amapolas,
centella
negra
del primer dolor,
estrella entre los peces,
a la luz
de la pura corriente genital,
ave morada del primer abismo,
sin alcoba, en el reino
del corazón visible
cuya miel inauguran los almendros,
el polen incendiario
de la retama agreste,
el toronjil de tentativas verdes,
la patria de los misteriosos musgos.

Sonaban las campanas de Cautín,
todos los pétalos pedían algo,
no renunciaba a nada la tierra,
el agua parpadeaba
sin cesar:
quería abrir el verano,   -
darle al fin una herida,
se despeñaba en furia
el río que venía de los Andes,
se convertía en una estrella dura
que clavaba la selva,
la orilla,
los peñascos:
allí no habita nadie:
sólo el agua y la tierra
y los trenes que aullaban,
los trenes del invierno
en sus ocupaciones

From **AMORES**

Terusa 1.

Terusa
who opened for me in the poppies,
black
bolt
of original grief,
star among fishes
in the sheer light
of a genital undertow,
swart bird of the primal abysses,
lacking even a bed sheet in that kingdom
of visible hearts
from whose honey the almond began,
the incendiary pollens
of the wilderness furze,
balsam of tentative greens
and the realms of ambiguous musk.

Bells rang in Cautín:
the petals were asking a question:
earth ceded nothing,
the water blinked like an eyelash
unceasingly.
I long to uncouple the summer,
stave through like a wound.
The river that rose in the Andes
flung its fury below,
then shrank to an obdurate star,
a nail driven into the forests,
the beaches,
the boulders.
No one came there to live: there was
only the water and land
and the keening of trains—
midwinter trains
at their task

atravesando el mapa
solitario:
reino mío,
reino de las raíces
con fulgor de menta,
cabellera de helechos,
pubis mojado,
reino de mi perdida pequeñez
cuando yo vi nacer la tierra
y yo formaba parte
de la mojada
integridad
terrestre:
lámpara entre los gérmenes y el agua,
en el nacimiento del trigo,
patria de las maderas
que morían
aullando en el aullido
de los aserraderos. . . .

Terusa,
inextinguible
aún en el olvido,
a traves
de las edades oxidadas,
aroma
señalado,
profunda madreselva o canto
o sueño
o luna que amasaron los jazmines
o amanecer del trébol junto al agua
o amplitud de la tierra con sus ríos
o demencia de flores o tristeza
o signo del imán o voluntad
del mar radiante y su baile infinito.

Rosaura 1.

Se aleja el navío del navío
haciendo las últimas señales

countercrossing the map's
solitude.
My place was
that kingdom of roots
smelling rankly of mint,
maidenhair in the ferns
and moist pubis,
the realm of my vanished minority.
I saw the soil teem
and I knew I was portion
of earth's
humid
integrity:
a lamp in the seeds and the water,
the thrust of the wheat
in a country of timber
that fell
under the scream
of the sawyer. . . .

Terusa,
immutably there
in oblivion,
in the rust
of the epochs
your distinctive
aroma persists,
rank honeysuckle, song
or a dream,
jasmine banked high by the moon,
trefoil of dawn by the water,
earth's breadth and its rivers,
a frenzy of flowers, despondency,
the mark of the magnet or the will
of the sea to be radiant and its dances, unending.

Rosaura 1.

The navies withdraw,
flashing their ultimate signals

en el sueño del mar,
de la marea
que vuelve a su planeta intransigente,
a su preocupación, a la limpieza:
queda la cama
en medio
de la hora infiel,
crepúsculo, azucena vespertina:
ya partieron los náufragos:
allí quedaron las sábanas rotas,
la embarcación
herida,
vamos mirando el Río Mapocho:
corre por él mi vida.

Rosaura de mi brazo,
va su vida en el agua,
el tiempo,
los tajamares de mampostería,
los puentes donde acuden
todos los pies cansados:
se va la ciudad por el río,
la luz por la corriente,
el corazón de barro
corre corre. . . .

Rosaura,
las habías olvidado
de tanto que volaban
en el humo:
allí se te olvidaron
en la esquina
de la calle Sazié, o en la plazuela
de Padura, en la picante rosa
del conventillo que nos compartía.
El minúsculo patio
guardó los excrementos
de los gatos errantes
y era una paz de bronce

on a somnolent sea,
the tides
turn back to their intransigent planet
and resume their pure work of ablution:
only the bed
in the midst of
the hour's infidelity
remains in its twilight, a crepuscular lily:
the shipwrecks have sailed off,
there are left us the splintering sheets
and the maimed embarkation;
we gaze out
toward the Río Mapocho,
my whole life awash in its passing.

Even here in my arms, Rosaura,
your lifetime streams out on the water,
time
and the backwaters that slip past the masonry,
the bridges where wearying feet
come and go in the world,
the eddying light
and the heart's murk—
all races on, races on. . . .

Rosaura,
you have forgotten
the world that flew off
in the smoke:
the corner
of Sazié Street and the square
of Padura, the acerb little rose
of a convent we divided,
no longer acknowledge you.
A minuscule courtyard
kept watch on the turds
of meandering cats;
a peace, as of bronze,

la que surgía
entre los dos desnudos:
la calma dura de los arrabales:
entre los párpados
nos caía el silencio
como un licor oscuro:
no dormíamos:
nos preparábamos para el amor:
habíamos gastado
el pavimento,
la fatiga,
el deseo,
y allí por fin estábamos
sueltos, sin ropa, sin ir y venir. . . .

Encendimos y apagamos el mundo,
tú te quedaste a oscuras:
yo seguí caminando los caminos,
rompiéndome las manos y los ojos,
dejé atrás el crepúsculo,
corté las amapolas vespertinas:
pasó un día que con su noche
procrearon
una nueva semana
y un año se durmió con otro año:
gota a gota
creció el tiempo,
hoja a hoja
el árbol transparente:
la ciudad polvorienta
cambió del agua al oro,
la guerra quemó pájaros y niños
en la Europa agobiada,
de Atacama el desierto
caminó con arena,
fuego y sal,
matando las raíces,
giraron en sus ácidos azules
los pálidos planetas,

rose from the two
of us, naked:
the implacable calm of the suburbs:
silence fell from our
eyelids,
like black brandy:
we had not come there to sleep:
we stripped down to make love:
after pounding
the pavements, worn down
by fatigue
and desire,
we peeled ourselves
free at last—no more comings and goings. . . .

We kindled and blew out the world:
while you kept to the shadows
I strode all the byways,
breaking my hands and my eyes;
leaving twilight behind,
I picked poppies at dusk:
day passed with its night,
on its way to a new week,
embracing,
one year went to sleep with another,
time
gathered,
drop after drop
and leaf over leaf,
a tree of transparency,
the dust of a city
turned the water to gold,
war calcified children and birds
in Europe's malignity;
in Atacama, a desert
moved off, sand,
fire and salt,
murdering roots;
the wan planets

tocó la luna un hombre,
cambió el pintor
y no pintó los rostros,
sino los signos y las cicatrices. . . .

whirled in their azures and acids,
a man hit the moon
and the painters found other vocations:
they painted faces no longer,
but scars, intimations, signs. . . .

AQUELLAS VIDAS

Éste soy, yo diré, para dejar
este pretexto escrito: ésta es mi vida.
Y ya se sabe que no se podía:
que en esta red no sólo el hilo cuenta,
sino el aire que escapa de las redes,
y todo lo demás era inasible:
el tiempo que corrió como una liebre
a través del rocío de Febrero
y más nos vale no hablar del amor
que se movía como una cadera
sin dejar donde estuvo tanto fuego
sino una cucharada de ceniza
y así con tantas cosas que volaban:
el hombre que esperó creyendo claro,
la mujer que vivió y que no vivirá,
todos pensaron que teniendo dientes,
teniendo pies y manos y alfabeto
era sólo cuestión de honor la vida.
Y éste sumó sus ojos a la historia,
agarró las victorias del pasado,
asumió para siempre la existencia
y sólo le sirvió para morir
la vida: el tiempo para no tenerlo.
Y la tierra al final para enterrarlo.

Pero aquello nació con tantos ojos
como planetas tiene el firmamento
y todo el fuego con que devoraba
la devoró sin tregua hasta dejarla.
Y si algo ví en mi vida fué una tarde
en la India, en las márgenes de un río:
arder una majer de carne y hueso
y no sé si era el alma o era el humo
lo que del sarcófago salía
hasta que no quedó mujer ni fuego
ni ataúd, ni ceniza: ya era tarde
y sólo noche y agua y sombra y río
allí permanecieron en la muerte.

"That's how I am," I'll say, leaving this
pretext in writing: "This is really my life."
But everyone knows that's not how it happens at all.
Not only the cords in the net, but the air
that escapes the interstices matters:
the rest remains as it was: inapprehensible.
Time races by like a hare
in the February dew.
As to love—love that unlimbers its haunches
leaving only a teaspoon of ashes
to say where the burning began—
the less said the better;
and the same for all mutable things: the man
who bided his time never doubting the outcome,
the woman who has lived out her time and will not come again—
all those who assume that, given the teeth in our head,
hands, feet and an alphabet,
life is only a matter of seeing things through with decorum.
One adds up the sum of his eyeballs and says it is history,
seizes the past and says it is glory,
believes that existence should go on forever,
and devotes his whole lifetime to
dying: empties all time of his living.
Earth shovels him under: it was worth little more, in the end.

Yet that man was born with eyes
like the planets that fill the whole firmament.
The fires he summoned to devour the thing that he wanted
burnt his lifetime away; he lived unappeased to the end.
But once in my life I saw plainly: one evening
in India; they were burning a woman
by the banks of a river, her bones and her body were burning:
I saw something move out of the burning sarcophagus
—call it smoke or a spirit—
till nothing was left of the fire or the woman
or the ash or the coffin. Evening had fallen.
There was night and the water, the dark
and the river, steadfast in that place and that dying.

AQUELLA LUZ

Esta luz de Ceylán me dió la vida,
me dió la muerte cuando yo vivía,
porque vivir adentro de un diamante
es solitaria escuela de enterrado,
es ser ave de pronto transparente,
araña que hila el cielo y se despide.

Esta luz de las islas me hizo daño,
me dejó para siempre circunspecto
como si el rayo de la miel remota
me sujetara al polvo de la tierra.

Llegué más extranjero que los pumas
y me alejé sin conocer a nadie
porque tal vez me trastornó los sesos
la luz occipital del paraíso.
(La luz que cae sobre el traje negro
y perfora la ropa y el decoro,
por eso desde entonces mi conflicto
es conservarme cada día desnudo.)

No entenderá tal vez el que no estuvo
tan lejos como yo para acercarse
ni tan perdido que ya parecía
un número nocturno de carbones.

Y entonces sólo pan y sólo luz.

Luz en el alma, luz en la cocina,
de noche luz y de mañana luz,
y luz entre las sábanas del sueño.
Hasta que amamantado de este modo
por la cruel claridad de mi destino
no tengo más remedio que vivir
entre desesperado y luminoso
sintiéndome tal vez desheredado
de aquellos reinos que no fueron míos.

THAT LIGHT

The light in Ceylon that was life to me
was death to me, too—for to live
in a diamond's intensity
is the lonely lyceum of corpses:
a bird made diaphanous
suddenly, a spider webbing the sky, and then gone.

Stung by the light of those islands,
I keep circumspect always,
as though a beam of that faraway
honey might turn me to ash in a moment.

More remote than the puma,
I moved out of range, knowing nobody,
dreading the occipital light of a paradise
that might one day explode in my brain.
(Light, falling on black, pierces more than the clothing—
it cuts through the wearer's decorum: I struggle
to live every day in an aura
of nakedness, now.)

Those never so wholly alone
in themselves, will not understand this, or come closer;
nor so lost as I seemed to be then,
a carbonized number at midnight.

There is left us the bread and the light.

The soul's light, and the light of the kitchen,
night light and the light of the morning,
light under the sheets of a dream.
Suckled by light,
I live as I must
in my destiny's ruthless lucidity,
between the luminous and the desperate halves,
disowned
by two kingdoms which never were mine.

Las redes que tiemblan en la luz
siguen saliendo claras del océano.

Toda la luz del tiempo permanece
y en su torre total el medio día.

Ahora todo me parece sombra.

The net cords that shake in the light
keep their clear intimation of ocean.

The sheer light of time is here with us still,
midday in its consummate tower.

All turns to darkness, it seems to me now.

NO HAY PURA LUZ

No hay pura luz
ni sombra en los recuerdos:
éstos se hicieron cárdena ceniza
o pavimento sucio
de calle atravesada por los pies de las gentes
que sin cesar salía y entraba en el mercado.

Y hay otros: los recuerdos buscando aún qué morder
como dientes de fiera no saciada.
Buscan, roen el hueso último, devoran
este largo silencio de lo que quedó atrás.

Y todo quedó atrás, noche y aurora,
el día suspendido como un puente entre sombras,
las cuidades, los puertos del amor y el rencor,
como si al almacén la guerra hubiera entrado
llevándose una a una todas las mercancías
hasta que a los vacíos anaqueles
llegue el viento a través de las puertas deshechas
y haga bailar los ojos del olvido.

Por eso a fuego lento surge la luz del día,
el amor, el aroma de una niebla lejana
y calle a calle vuelve la ciudad sin banderas
a palpitar tal vez y a vivir en el humo.

Horas de ayer cruzadas por el hilo
de una vida como por una aguja sangrienta
entre las decisiones sin cesar derribadas,
el infinito golpe del mar y de la duda
y la palpitación del cielo y sus jazmines.

Quién soy Aquél? Aquel que no sabía
sonreír, y de puro enlutado moría?
Aquel que el cascabel y el clavel de la fiesta
sostuvo derrocando la cátedra del frío?

THE LIGHT IS NOT PURE

Those pure lights
and darks are not memory's:
the glowering light in the coal
is memory's, the filth of the
paving stone, streets broken by footsteps
of comers and goers interminably there in the market place.

And those others: the biters and predators, thoughts
like a beast's tooth, the implacable ones
stalking an ultimate bone, the scavengers gnawing away
at the infinite silence of all we had left in the past.

All falls behind us: sunrises, nights,
day like a bridge's suspensions, spanning the shadows,
cities, the seaports to rancor and love:
the heat of the battle has found out the warehouses,
lock, stock and barrel, and borne our possessions away,
till only the wind's sound remains
in a world of stripped lockers and overthrown doors
and oblivion's eye dances off.

Day seethes on its simmering fires and brims over,
love, or the smell of a faraway cloud,
street after street where a city comes back, without banners,
trembles to life again, it may be, and lives in the haze.

Yesterday's hours, threading
our lives, as though with the blood of a needle,
between decisions ceaselessly whittled away,
the infinite shock of the sea, the misgivings,
the shaking of jasmine and sky.

Who is that Other I am? He who never
contrived how to smile and died of his perfect deprival?
Who outlasted the festival bells and the gala
carnation, and toppled the lecterns of cold?

Pablo Neruda / 211

Es tarde, tarde. Y sigo. Sigo con un ejemplo
tras otro, sin saber cuál es la moraleja,
porque de tantas vidas que tuve estoy ausente
y soy, a la vez soy aquel hombre que fuí.

Tal vez es este el fin, la verdad misteriosa.

La vida, la continua sucesión de un vacío
que de día y de sombra llenaban esta copa
y el fulgor fué enterrado como un antiguo príncipe
en su propia mortaja de mineral enfermo,
hasta que tan tardíos ya somos, que no somos:
ser y no ser resultan ser la vida.

De lo que fuí no tengo sino estas marcas crueles
porque aquellos dolores confirman mi existencia.

Late, it grows late. I go on with it all. I pursue
this or that paradigm, never guessing the answer,
knowing myself, in each of the lives I have lived,
both absent and present, at once the man who I was, and I am.

Does the rub of mysterious verity lie there?

The whole of a lifetime, the persisting successions of vacancy
brimming our cup with its daylight and dark,
while a luster is borne underground, antiquity's princeling
in his natural graveclothes of sickening mineral,
until we are tardily there, too late to be there at all:
being and not being, life takes its being from these.

Of whatever I was, I hold only these cruel lacerations
and so confirm my existence, confirmed in its woe.

DESLUMBRA EL DÍA

Nada para los ojos del invierno,
ni una lágrima más,
hora por hora se arma verde
la estación esencial, hoja por hoja,
hasta que con su nombre nos llamaron
para participar de la alegría.

Qué bueno es el eterno *para todos*,
el aire limpio, la promesa flor:
la luna llena deja
su carta en el follaje:
hombre y mujer vuelven del mar
con un cesto mojado
de plata en movimiento.

Como amor o medalla
yo recibo,
recibo
del Sur, del Norte, del violín,
del perro,
del limón, de la greda,
del aire recién puesto en libertad,
recibo máquinas de aroma oscuro
mercaderías color de tormenta,
todo lo necesario:
azahares, cordeles,
uvas como topacios,
olor de ola:
yo acumulo
sin tregua,
sin trabajo,
respiro,
seco al viento mi traje,
mi corazón desnudo,
y cae,
cae el cielo:
en una copa
bebo
la alegría.

A DAZZLING DAY

Nothing more for those wintering eyes—
not a tear more!
The hours, in essential succession,
gird their green armory, leaf after leaf,
and call to us here in their name
to inherit felicity.

How good, that eternal *For all and for each!*
clean air, with a promise of flowers;
the full moon leaves
its card in the foliage:
men and women return from the sea
with drenched baskets
of mercurial silver.

I take it all in,
like love or a lover's medallion;
I take to myself
the gifts of the South and the North, the dog
and the fiddle,
lemon and chalk
and all that is newly unleashed on the air:
machines with their quizzical smell,
a storm-colored merchandise
—whatever is needful:
lengths of cord and the flowering orange,
grapes with their topazes,
the smell of a wave:
I gather them all
without stint or
exertion,
I breathe out,
dry my clothes in the wind
and my heart's nakedness;
the sky falls
and falls:
I drink happiness
there
in that cup.

III: El cruel fuego

MAREAS

Crecí empapado en aguas naturales
como el molusco en fósforo marino:
en mí repercutía la sal rota
y mi propio esqueleto construía.
Cómo explicar, casi sin movimiento
de la respiración azul y amarga,
una a una las olas repitieron
lo que yo presentía y palpitaba
hasta que sal y zumo me formaron:
el desdén y el deseo de una ola,
el ritmo verde que en lo más oculto
levantó un edificio transparente,
aquel secreto se mantuvo y luego
sentí que yo latía como aquello:
que mi canto crecía con el agua.

III: The Cruel Fire

THE TIDES

Drenched in my natural waters, I came of age
like the mollusk in nautical phosphor;
salts broke and rebounded in me,
contrived the device of my intimate skeleton.
How give it a name—something almost
unmoved in itself, in the blue, bitter breathing
that gave back to me, wave after wave,
my unique intimations; that seethed
and then bodied me forth in the brine and the resin:
the disdain and desire of a wave,
green rhythm at the heart of a mystery
that raised a diaphanous mansion;
a secret reserved to itself that I later
sensed as my own, like a pulse beat made mine,
till my song came of age, with the water.

EL MAR

Necesito del mar porque me enseña:
no sé si aprendo música o conciencia:
no sé si es ola sola o ser profundo
o sólo ronca voz o deslumbrante
suposición de peces y navíos.
El hecho es que hasta cuando estoy dormido
de algún modo magnético circulo
en la universidad del oleaje.

No son sólo las conchas trituradas
como si algún planeta tembloroso
participara paulatina muerte,
no, del fragmento reconstruyo el día,
de una racha de sal la estalactita
y de una cucharada el dios inmenso.

Lo que antes me enseñó lo guardo! Es aire,
incesante viento, agua y arena.

Parece poco para el hombre joven
que aquí llegó a vivir con sus incendios,
y sin embargo el pulso que subía
y bajaba a su abismo,
el frío del azul que crepitaba,
el desmoronamiento de la estrella,
el tierno desplegarse de la ola
despilfarrando nieve con la espuma,
el poder quieto, allí, determinado
como un trono de piedra en lo profundo,
sustituyó el recinto en que crecían
tristeza terca, amontonando olvido,
y cambió bruscamente mi existencia:
di mi adhesión al puro movimiento.

THE SEA

I need an ocean to teach me:
whatever it is that I learn—music or consciousness,
the single wave in the sea, the abyss of my being,
the guttural rasp of my voice, or the blazing
presumption of fishes and navies—
so much is certain: even in sleep, as if
by the trick of a magnet, I spin on the circle
of wave upon wave of the sea, the sea's university.

More than the mash of the sea-conch, as though
worn by a planet's vibrations
that dies by degrees,
I salvage the day with a fragment,
restore the stalactite with a volley of salt
and spoon up a godhead's immensity.

And all that I learn is remembered. It is air,
it is sand, it is water, the interminable wind.

The young think it little,
coming to live here with their fires;
yet out of those recesses where a pulse once
ascended or sank to its void,
the crackle and freeze of the blue,
a star's granulation,
the tender deployment of waves
that squander their snow on the foam,
the reticent power, undeflectable,
a stone throne on the deep,
my wayward despondency, heaping oblivion higher,
turned, until suddenly all my existence was changed:

and I cling with the whole of my being to what is purest in
movement.

SOLILOQUIO EN LAS OLAS

Sí, pero aquí estoy solo.
Se levanta
una ola
tal vez dice su nombre, no comprendo,
murmura, arrastra el peso
de espuma y movimiento
y se retira. A quién
preguntaré lo que me dijo?
A quién entre las olas
podré nombrar?
Y espero.

Otra vez se acercó la claridad,
se levantó en la espuma
el dulce número
y no supe nombrarlo.
Así cayó el susurro:
se deslizó a la boca de la arena:
el tiempo destruyó todos los labios
con la paciencia
de la sombra y el
beso anaranjado
del verano.
Yo me quedé solo
sin poder acudir a lo que el mundo,
sin duda, me ofrecía,
oyendo
cómo se desgranaba la riqueza,
las misteriosas uvas
de la sal, el amor desconocido
y quedaba en el día degradado
sólo un rumor
cada vez más distante
hasta que todo lo que pudo ser
se convirtió en silencio.

Yes, but it's lonely here.
The wave builds
and breaks, speaking
its name, it may be: I understand nothing.
A murmur arises, dragging its weight
in the foam and flotation,
falls back again. Who's to say
what it says to me there?
Whom shall I call
from the wave?
I wait.

Another time, clarity
falls very close: the sweet number
heaves up in the spray
but I cannot decipher it.
Like a sigh moving down from the air:
a slithering mouth in the sand:
time wrecks all the lips
with the patience
of darkness, the
tangerine kiss
of the summer.
Bereft and alone,
I go numb to the manifest
grace of the world,
hearing
some bounty that batters itself into bits,
mysterious grapes
in the salt, love undisclosed;
until only a rumor
remains of the day's degradation,
each moment more distant,
and the imminent gift of the possible
turns wholly toward silence.

Pablo Neruda / *221*

IV: El cazador de raices

EL HÉROE

Me convidó la dueña del castillo
a cada habitación para llorar.
Yo no la conocía
pero la amaba con amor amargo
como si mis desdichas se debieran
a que una vez dejó caer sus trenzas
sobre mí, derramándome la sombra.

Ahora ya era tarde.

Entramos
entre los retratos muertos,
y las pisadas
eran
como
si fuéramos tocando
hacia abajo
a la puerta
del triste honor, del laberinto ciego,
y la única verdad
era el olvido.

Por eso, en cada estancia
el silencio era un líquido,
y la señora dura del castillo
y yo, el testigo negro,
vacilábamos juntos
flotando en aquel frío,
tocaba el techo con su cabellera:
arriba el oro sucio
de los viejos salones
se confundía con sus pies desnudos.

El espeso sigilo
de las caducas cámaras

IV: The Root-Hunter

THE HERO

The castle keep's lady
led on through the hallways, lamenting.
Unknown to each other,
my love followed her bitterly,
as if all my disasters were pledged
to some power in the past that had loosened
its braids over me and drowned me in darkness.

It began to grow later.

We went in
among the slain pictures;
our footsteps
fell strangely
as if,
far below us,
we struck
at the door
of our mourning integrity, blind in a labyrinth
where only oblivion
was sure.

At the landings
the silence was liquid:
the castle's implacable lady
and I, her dark witness,
wavered forward
afloat in the cold;
her hair grazed the ceiling:
above, the soiled gold
of old passageways
touched her feet's nakedness, and merged.

The packed crests
on the moldering bedchambers

me levantaba, pero yo luché
invocando la naturalidad
de la física pura,
pero la castellana sumergida
me invitó a continuar
y divagando
sobre las alfombras rotas,
llorando en los pasillos,
llegaron horas puras y vacías,
sin alimentación y sin palabras,
o todo era pasado o sueño vano,
o el tiempo
no nos reconocía
y en su red, presos como peces, éramos
dos condenados al castillo inmóvil.

Aquellas horas sostengo en mis manos
como se guardan piedras o cenizas
sin pedir nada más a los recuerdos.
Pero, si mi destino errante
me conduce a los muros del castillo,
me cubro con mi máscara,
apresuro
el paso junto al foso,
cruzo las márgenes del funesto lago,
me alejo sin mirar: tal vez sus trenzas
caigan una vez más de los balcones
y ella con llanto agudo
llegue a mi corazón a detenerme.

Por eso yo, el astuto cazador
camino enmascarado por el bosque.

bore me up: I gathered my will
to strike back,
invoking the physical
force of the world:
but the castle keep's lady,
sinking ever more deeply, beckoned me on,
veering this way and that
on the raveling carpets,
weeping in corridors;
hours lapsed, empty and flawless,
without speech or sustenance,
all was lost in the past, or an impotent dream,
time no longer
acknowledged us,
our fate was to live in the castle's immobility,
like fish in the cords of a net.

My hands hold the hours
like a fistful of ashes or pebbles;
I ask nothing of memory.
But should a fugitive destiny
lead me once more to those battlements,
I shall strike
through my covering mask
for the pass by the moat,
ford the edge of the lachrymose water,
and take cover: there, it may be,
the braids will unfold from the balconies,
the lady prodigious in grief
will lay hands on my heart, to detain me.

Circumspect hunter, in that hope
I walked masked through the forest.

EL CAZADOR EN EL BOSQUE

Al bosque mío entro con raíces,
con mi fecundidad: De dónde
vienes? me pregunta
una hoja verde y ancha como un mapa.
Yo no respondo. Allí
es húmedo el terreno
y mis botas se clavan, buscan algo,
golpean para que abran,
pero la tierra calla.

Callará hasta que yo comience a ser
sustancia muerta y viva, enredadera,
feroz tronco del árbol erizado
o copa temblorosa.

Calla la tierra para que no sepan
sus nombres diferentes, ni su extendido idioma,
calla porque trabaja
recibiendo y naciendo:
cuanto muere recoge
como una anciana hambrienta:
todo se pudre en ella,
hasta la sombra,
el rayo,
los duros esqueletos,
el agua, la ceniza,
todo se une al rocío,
a la negra llovizna
de la selva.

El mismo sol se pudre
y el oro interrumpido
que le arroja
cae en el saco de la selva y pronto
se fundió en la amalgama, se hizo harina,
y su contribución resplandeciente
se oxidó como un arma abandonada.

HUNTER IN THE FOREST

I enter my forest in my roots
and my plenitude: "Where
are you from?" a leaf
lavish and green as a map, asks me.
I have nothing to say. The clay
wets my boot soles and
clings: something is wanting: they
beat on the forest floor, as if
seeking an opening: but the earth remains silent.

Nothing will alter that stillness but
a changing of substances, my living and dying, a
climber alive on a tree trunk's ferocity, bristling
its tendrils, or a tremulous cup.

Earth remains silent: it will never
divulge all its names, or its gamut
of languages; receiving,
conceiving, it toils and says nothing:
whatever perishes, it takes
with a hag's hunger:
there all decomposes—
scintillation
and shadow,
the refractory skeleton,
cinder and water—
all join in a dewdrop
or the drizzle that blackens
the forest.

Even the sun rots;
the extortionate gold
in the rock soon
falls into the pouch of the forest, turns
into an alloy, or dissolves into meal:
its flashing beneficence
rusts in a junkpile of armor.

Pablo Neruda / 227

Vengo a buscar raíces,
las que hallaron
el alimento mineral del bosque,
la substancia
tenaz, el zinc sombrío,
el cobre venenoso.

Esa raíz debe nutrir mi sangre.

Otra encrespada, abajo,
es parte poderosa
del silencio,
se impone como paso de reptil:
avanza devorando,
toca el agua, la bebe,
y sube por el árbol
la orden secreta:
sombrío es el trabajo
para que las estrellas sean verdes.

Root-hunter, I come
searching for things
that nourish the ores of the forest,
all the obdurate
substances, the spleen in the zinc
and the poisonous copper.

In this root my blood prospers.

All the rest, braiding under me,
is the ponderous portion
of silence:
like the track of the saurian,
it lumbers ahead and devours
what it touches, it takes hold and it drinks up
the streams, it ascends in the tree
in its secret decorum: unseen,
the work of the earth remains somber,
that the stars may be green.

LA NOCHE

Entro en el aire negro.
La noche viaja, tiene
paciencia en su follaje,
se mueve
con su espacio,
redonda,
agujereada,
con qué plumas se envuelve?
O va desnuda?
Cayó sobre metálicas
montañas
cubriéndolas con sal
de estrellas duras:
uno por uno
cuanto monte
existe
se extinguió y descendió bajo sus alas:
bajo el trabajo negro de sus manos.
Al mismo tiempo
fuimos
barro negro,
muñecos
derribados
que dormían
sin ser, dejando fuera al traje diurno,
las lanzas de oro, el sombrero de espigas,
la vida con sus calles y sus números
allí quedó,
montón de pobre orgullo,
colmena sin sonido,
Ay noche y noche abierta
boca, barca, botella,
no sólo tiempo y sombra,
no sólo la fatiga,
algo irrumpe, se colma
como una taza,
leche oscura,

NIGHT

I come into black air.
Night, on its way, takes its time
in the foliage,
moves
into its spaces,
rounding
and piercing.
How shall she feather her forms?
Or shall she go naked?
Night falls on the metal
of mountains,
covers the heights with the vehement
salt of stars:
one by one
she puts out
the mountains
or gathers them under her wings:
black work for her fingers.
All at once
we are
black
bog water,
smashed
dolls
asleep in non-being leaving behind us
a habit of clothing, our gold-pointed lances, our corn-tassel
hats—the life of the streets and the house numbers:
all that beggarly pomp heaped high
like a beehive of silence
in back of us.
And night, night opens totally—
boats, bottles, and mouths—
more
than time and the darkness
or our singular weariness, it
erupts and brims over,
a cup of

Pablo Neruda / 231

sal negra,
y cae
adentro
de su pozo
el destino,
se quema cuanto existe, el humo
viaja buscando espacio hasta extender la noche,
pero
de la ceniza
mañana
naceremos.

inscrutable milk,
black brine
flowing down
to that
well
where the will of the world
burns all that exists to a crisp. The smoke
widens, forces the spaces, enlarges the night;
but
out of those ashes
tomorrow
we issue once more to the world.

CITA DE INVIERNO

III

Quién no desea un alma dura?
Quién no se practicó en el alma un filo?
Cuando a poco de ver vimos el odio
y de empezar a andar nos tropezaron
y de querer amar nos desamaron
y sólo de tocar fuimos heridos,
quién no hizo algo por armar sus manos
y para subsistir hacerse duro
como el cuchillo, y devolver la herida?
El delicado pretendió aspereza,
el más tierno buscaba empuñadura,
el que sólo quería que lo amaran
con un tal vez, con la mitad de un beso,
pasó arrogante sin mirar a aquella
que lo esperaba abierta y desdichada:
no hubo nada que hacer: de calle en calle
se establecieron mercados de máscaras
y el mercader probaba a cada uno
un rostro de crepúsculo o de tigre,
de austero, de virtud, de antepasado,
hasta que terminó la luna llena
y en la noche sin luz fuimos iguales.

WINTER ENCOUNTER

III

Who does not hope for a perdurable heart
or hone the cold edge of his spirit?
With eyes barely opened, we see the world's hatred,
tottering into the world, we fall on our faces,
hoping for love, we find the world slack in its loving,
touching with tentative hands, we wince under our wounds:
knowing these things, who would not look to his weaponry,
temper himself for survival,
or live like a knife blade, returning one wound for another?
The finicky brazen it out with a show of bravado,
those with the tenderest skins reach for their holsters,
while those who would settle for love,
midway in a kiss, with an arrogant
take-it-or-leave-it, pass the luckless and credulous
by, without once looking back.
So wags the world: up hill and down dale
they set up their tables and peddled their masquerades,
the pitchman was there with a different mask for each comer—
a crepuscular mask, or the face of a tiger, the masks
of austerity, piety, family pedigree—
till the full moon moved out of its quarter
and pitch-black in the darkness, we all looked the same.

EL PESCADOR

Con larga lanza el pescador desnudo
ataca al pez pegado al roquerío
el mar el aire el hombre están inmóviles
tal vez como una rosa la piedad
se abre al borde del agua y sube lenta
deteniendo en silencio la dureza
parece que uno a uno los minutos
se replegaron como un abanico
y el corazón del pescador desnudo
tranquilizó en el agua su latido
pero cuando la roca no miraba
y la ola olvidaba sus poderes
en el centro de aquel planeta mudo
se descargó el relámpago del hombre
contra la vida inmóvil de la piedra
clavó la lanza en la materia pura
el pez herido palpitó en la luz
cruel bandera del mar indiferente
mariposa de sal ensangrentada.

FISHERMAN

With the length of his lance the stripped fisherman
assaults the stricken fish in the rockery
man ocean and air keep immobile
compassion it may be divides
like a rose on the waterline mounts slowly
draws into its silence the unbreakable world
moment for moment it may be
all unfolds like a fan
the nude fisherman's heart
steadies its beat in the sea and is tranquil
when everything alters the rock looks toward nothing
the breaker forgets its ferocity
and the bolt in the fist of the man
is aimed at a stilled planet's center
strikes the immovable life of the stone
sinks a lance in primordial matter
the hurt fish shudders in radiance
ocean's unpitying flag indifferent now
a butterfly in a bloodbath of salt.

DE PRONTO UNA BALADA

Será verdad que otra vez ha golpeado
como aroma o temor, como extranjero
que no conoce bien calle ni casa.
Será verdad, tan tarde, y luego aún
la vida manifiesta una ruptura
algo nace en el fondo de lo que era
ceniza
y el vaso tiembla con el nuevo vino
que cae y que lo enciende. Ay! será aquello
igual que ayer, camino sin señales,
y las estrellas arden con frescura
de jazmines entre tú y la noche,
ay! es algo que asume la alegría
atropelladamente rechazada
y que declara sin que nadie escuche
que no se rinde. Y sube una bandera
una vez más a las torres quemadas.
Oh amor oh amor de pronto y de amenaza,
súbito, oscurecido, se estremece
la memoria y acude
el navío de plata,
el desembarcadero matutino:
niebla y espuma cubren las riberas,
cruza un grito espacial hacia las islas
y en plena puerta herida del Océano
la novia con su cola de azucenas
lista para partir. Mira sus trenzas:
son dos cascadas puras de carbones,
dos alas negras como golondrinas,
dos pesadas cadenas victoriosas.
Y ella como en la cita de esponsales
aguarda coronada por el mar
en el embarcadero imaginario.

SUDDEN BALLAD

Truth will come knocking
another time, like a smell or a tremor, a stranger
unsure of the street and the house number.
Truth ever so tardily there:
in the midst of the breaking of lives
something is born in the pit of the
cinder,
new wine in the sputtering glass
brimming and burning. Oh, yesterday's truth
is unchanged—the pathway unmarked by a sign,
the stars in their places, ablaze
in the freshening jasmine, between you and the night:
something that happiness wrought
out of panic denial
and declared to the world, unheard
and unhumbled. A flag flies again
from the towers in a holocaust.
Love, love, love, love—the warnings are suddenly there,
unforeseen and obscure, and all we remember
flows forth, the navies of silver
and the dawn's debarkation.
Mist and foam blind the beaches,
space calls to the islands, crosses over
where the bride at the sea-stricken
door, plaiting her hair with a lily,
waits to embark. See how the braids
fall, two cascades of immaculate coal,
two wings black as swallows,
two chains with the weight of their victory:
the betrothed in the tryst of the harbor,
crowned with an ocean,
with the setting-forth only imagined.

V: Sonata crítica

LA MEMORIA

Tengo que acordarme de todo,
recoger las briznas, los hilos
del acontecer harapiento
y metro a metro las moradas,
los largos caminos del tren,
la superficie del dolor.

Si se me extravía un rosal
y confundo noche con liebre
o bien se me desmoronó
todo un muro de la memoria
tengo que hacer de nuevo el aire,
el vapor, la tierra, las hojas,
el pelo y también los ladrillos,
las espinas que me clavaron,
la velocidad de la fuga.

Tengan piedad para el poeta.

Siempre olvidé con avidez
y en aquellas manos que tuve
sólo cabían inasibles
cosas que no se tocaban,
que se podían comparar
sólo cuando ya no existían.

Era el humo como un aroma,
era el aroma como el humo,
la piel de un cuerpo que dormía
y que despertó con mis besos,
pero no me pidan la fecha
ni el nombre de lo que soñé,
ni puedo medir el camino
que tal vez no tiene país

V: Critical Sonata

MEMORY

All must be remembered:
a turning wind, the threads
in the threadbare event must be gathered,
yard after yard of all we inhabited,
the train's long trajectory,
and the trappings of sorrow.

Should a rosebush be lost
or the hare's track dissolve in the night,
should the pillars of memory
topple out of my reach,
I must remake the air,
the steam and the soil and the leaves,
my skin or the bricks in the wall,
the thorn in my flesh
and the haste of my flight.

Pity the poor poet!

I was always an avid forgetter:
in my two human hands
only the untouchable things of the world
live unscathed,
and the power of comparison
is the sum of their total destruction.

Smoke came like a smell,
and smell passed like a smoke,
the skin of a body asleep
that woke to my kisses:
no one asked for the date
or the name of my dream;
I am powerless to measure the road
that leads to no country, perhaps,

o aquella verdad que cambió
que tal vez se apagó de día
y fué luego luz errante
como en la noche una luciérnaga.

or the truth's pure mutation
that might blow itself out in the daylight
or change to the glow
of a firefly's vagary at night.

EL LARGO DÍA JUEVES

Apenas desperté reconocí
el día, era el de ayer,
era el día de ayer con otro nombre,
era un amigo que creí perdido
y que volvía para sorprenderme.

Jueves, le dije, espérame,
voy a vestirme y andaremos juntos
hasta que tú te caigas en la noche.
Tú morirás, yo seguiré
despierto, acostumbrado
a las satisfacciones de la sombra.

Las cosas ocurrieron de otro modo
que contaré con íntimos detalles.

Tardé en llenarme de jabón el rostro
—qué deliciosa espuma
en mis mejillas—
sentí como si el mar me regalara
blancura sucesiva
mi cara fué sólo un islote oscuro
rodeado por ribetes de jabón
y cuando en el combate
de las pequeñas olas y lamidos
del tierno hisopo y la afilada hoja
fuí torpe y de inmediato,
malherido,
malgasté las toallas
con gotas de mi sangre,
busqué alumbre, algodón, yodo, farmacias
completas que corrieron a mi auxilio:
sólo acudió mi rostro en el espejo,
mi cara mal lavada y mal herida.

El baño
me incitaba

LONG DAY'S THURSDAY

Barely awake, I remembered
what day it was: it was yesterday's
day, or yesterday by some other name,
my long-lost compadre
come back to surprise me.

Thursday, I said: wait up for me,
I'll get into my clothes, we'll
go out on the town till you drop in your tracks,
I'm with you, right to the end,
wide awake, favoring the dark side,
as usual.

But what really happened was this:
in intimate detail:

There I was with a faceful of shaving soap,
a touch behind schedule—my cheeks
in a succulent bubble bath—
when all at once I felt wave after wave
of the whiteness pass over me, like the
sea giving presents:
there was nothing left of my face but this strange little
island, surrounded by streamers of soap,
with little driblets and ripples
of tremulous hyssop slamming into each other,
and my razor blade ready;
I went limp—the next minute
here I was bleeding to death,
slopping the towels
with my blood,
looking for iodine, cotton, spirits of alum—
a whole drugstore: first aid to the wounded;
there was only this face looking back from the shaving glass,
my face, half unwashed and nicked into hamburger.

Then the bathtub
called out to me,

con prenatal calor a sumergirme
y acurruqué mi cuerpo en la pereza.

Aquella cavidad intrauterina
me dejó agazapado
esperando nacer, inmóvil, líquido,
substancia temblorosa
que participa de la inexistencia
y demoré en moverme
horas enteras,
estirando las piernas con delicia
bajo la submarina caloría.

Cuánto tiempo en frotarme y en secarme,
cuánto una media después de otra media
y medio pantalón y otra mitad,
tan largo trecho me ocupó un zapato
que cuando en dolorosa incertidumbre
escogí la corbata, y ya partía
de exploración, buscando mi sombrero,
comprendí que era demasiado tarde:
la noche había llegado
y comencé de nuevo a desnudarme,
prenda por prenda, a entrar entre las sábanas,
hasta que pronto me quedé dormido.

Cuando pasó la noche y por la puerta
entró otra vez el Jueves anterior
correctamente transformado en Viernes
lo saludé con risa sospechosa,
con desconfianza por su identidad.
Espérame, le dije, manteniendo
puertas, ventanas plenamente abiertas,
y comencé de nuevo mi tarea
de espuma de jabón hasta sombrero,
pero mi vano esfuerzo
se encontró con la noche que llegaba
exactamente cuando yo salía.
Y volví a desvestirme con esmero.

prenatally tepid: submerge!
so I settled myself in for a doze.

In that uterine cavity
I let everything go, crouched
in a birth position, immobile, liquescent,
a quivering jelly
quite at home in its new nonexistence,
not moving a muscle
for hours on end,
dilating my legs blissfully
in the submarine calories.

I took time drying and rubbing myself down,
one half of me first, then the other,
then one trouser leg and the other;
just getting into my shoes seemed to go on forever;
when it came to the choice of a tie
in my doleful uncertainty and looking around for
my hat, after due exploration
I saw it was already too late:
it was nighttime again,
I started to peel off my clothes again,
item by item, I went back to the sheets; next thing
I was dead to the world.

Another night passed, and
the Thursday-before-that came in the front door again,
correctly transformed into Friday.
We greeted and smiled, but a part of me
wondered suspiciously: wasn't this somebody else, some impostor?
Wait up for me, friend, I said—keeping
everything, windows and doors, all the way open;
and once more I began the whole bit
with the soap bubbles, right on through to the hat;
I missed out again:
before I knew it, all set to take off for the day,
I found it was night again.
So I docilely slipped out of my clothes.

Pablo Neruda / 247

Mientras tanto esperando en la oficina
los repugnantes expedientes, los
números que volaban al papel
como mínimas aves migratorias
unidas en despliegue amenazante.
Me pareció que todo se juntaba
para esperarme por primera vez:
el nuevo amor que, recién descubierto,
bajo un árbol del parque me incitaba
a continuar en mí la primavera.

Y mi alimentación fué descuidada
día tras día, empeñado en ponerme
uno tras otro mis aditamentos,
en lavarme y vestirme cada día.
Era una insostenible situación:
cada vez un problema la camisa,
más hostiles las ropas interiores
y más interminable la chaqueta.

Hasta que poco a poco me morí
de inanición, de no acertar, de nada,
de estar entre aquel día que volvía
y la noche esperando como viuda.

Ya cuando me morí todo cambió.

Bien vestido, con perla en la corbata,
y ya exquisitamente rasurado
quise salir, pero no había calle,
no había nadie en la calle que no había,
y por lo tanto nadie me esperaba.

Y el Jueves duraría todo el año.

Meanwhile, all manner of nasty
contingencies were waiting for me in the office—the
numbers that fly over papers
like pint-sized migrations
coming over in menacing waves.
Everything possible ganged up for its
very first visit and was waiting to see me,
it seemed: my new pickup under the trees
in the park was leading me on
as if I could make the whole spring happen.

My digestion went haywire,
day after day I was busy with details,
one thing or another, all the extras,
washing and dressing myself and the rest of it.
It was really too much:
over and over again, that problem with shirts,
the wholly hostile behavior of my shorts and my underthings
and the endless to-do about jackets.

Little by little, I was wasting away
in my own inanition, my quandaries, my
nothingness, pinned down, as I was, between one day
coming up and night waiting out there like a widow.

Then I died; and everything changed for the better.

Dressed up like a clotheshorse, with a pearl in my
necktie, and for once, irreproachably shaved,
I was all set for a night on the town—when, imagine,
someone pulled in the streets, there was nobody there on the
streets, they had ceased to exist and nobody was waiting.

And Thursday might well go on being Thursday all the year long.

NO ES NECESARIO

No es necesario silbar
para estar solo,
para vivir a oscuras.

En plena muchedumbre, a pleno cielo,
nos recordamos a nosotros mismos,
al íntimo, al desnudo,
al único que sabe cómo crecen sus uñas,
que sabe cómo se hace su silencio
y sus pobres palabras.
Hay Pedro para todos,
luces, satisfactorias Berenices,
pero, adentro,
debajo de la edad y de la ropa,
aún no tenemos nombre,
somos de otra manera.
No sólo por dormir los ojos se cerraron
sino para no ver el mismo cielo.
Nos cansamos de pronto
y como si tocaran la campana
para entrar al colegio,
regresamos al pétalo escondido,
al hueso, a la raíz semi secreta
y allí, de pronto, somos,
somos aquello puro y olvidado,
somos lo verdadero
entre los cuatro muros de nuestra única piel,
entre las dos espadas de vivir y morir.

NO ONE NEED WHISTLE

No one need whistle
to live to himself
and keep in the shadow.

In the crush of a multitude or the open light of the day
we remember: we think of ourselves,
the nude and the intimate one,
he who knows how his fingernails lengthen,
how to order his silences
and contrive his poor speech out of words.
The Pedros live on,
and the lights, and the satisfactory Berenices,
yet always within us
under the birthdays and clothing
we know ourselves nameless
and call ourselves alien.
Shutting our eyes, we ask more than a habit of slumber:
we long to efface the identical sky.
And we suddenly tire of it all;
like schoolboys
whom the summoning bell rings indoors,
we go back to the stealth of the petal,
the bone, the half-secret of roots—
and then all at once we are there:
the forgotten, the purest in heart,
undissembled,
between four walls of unmatchable skin
and two blades of our living and dying.

Pablo Neruda / 251

LA VERDAD

Os amo idealismo y realismo,
como agua y piedra
sois
partes del mundo,
luz y raíz del árbol de la vida.

No me cierren los ojos
aún después de muerto,
los necesitaré aún para aprender,
para mirar y comprender mi muerte.

Necesita mi boca
para cantar después, cuando no exista.
Y mi alma y mis manos y mi cuerpo
para seguirte amando, amada mía.

Sé que no puede ser, pero esto quise.

Amo lo que no tiene sino sueños.

Tengo un jardín de flores que no existen.

Soy decididamente triangular.

Aún echo de menos mis orejas,
pero las enrollé para dejarlas
en un puerto fluvial del interior
de la República de Malagueta.

No puedo más con la razón al hombro.

Quiero inventar el mar de cada día.

Vino una vez a verme
un gran pintor que pintaba soldados.
Todos eran heroicos y el buen hombre

THE TRUTH

Realism, idealism: how I dote on you both,
like water and rock,
both
parts of my world,
light and the tree of life packing its roots underground.

And I pray that my eyes never shut,
even for death:
I who need all my vision to learn,
see at first hand, and interpret my dying.

Need my mouth
to sing in the aftermath when the mouth comes to nothing:
my body as well as my soul, and the arms
that replenish our loving, beloved, as before.

All of it hopeless, I know—but I dote on it still.

Whatever has whittled itself down to a dream.

A garden I tend whose blossom never existed.

I keep steadfastly triangular.

Needing ears,
I tighten the whorls of my hearing and leave them
upriver somewhere in the deepest interior
of Free Malagueta.

So much for notional man and the life of pure reason.

I would rather invent the sea's dailiness.

I'd a friend, a fine painter,
a painter of soldiers,
heroical, all of them—or so it appeared

Pablo Neruda / 253

los pintaba en el campo de batalla
muriéndose de gusto.

También pintaba vacas realistas
y eran tan extremadamente vacas
que uno se iba poniendo melancólico
y dispuestos a rumiar eternamente.

Execración y horror! Leí novelas
interminablemente bondadosas
y tantos versos sobre
el Primero de Mayo
que ahora escribo sólo sobre el 2 de ese mes.

Parece ser que el hombre
atropella el paisaje
y ya la carretera que antes tenía cielo
ahora nos agobia
con su empecinamiento comercial.

Así suele pasar con la belleza
como si no quisiéramos comprarla
y la empaquetan a su gusto y modo.

Hay que dejar que baile la belleza
con los galanes más inaceptables,
entre el día y la noche:
no la obliguemos a tomar la píldora
de la verdad como una medicina.

Y lo real? También, sin duda alguna,
pero que nos aumente,
que nos alargue, que nos haga fríos,
que nos redacte
tanto el orden del pan como el del alma.

A susurrar! ordeno
al bosque puro,

on the good fellow's canvas: all expiring
on battlefields, and expiring with unction.

He could paint representational cows
when he chose, the cow-in-itself, so wholly rendered as cow
that one sickened of long rumination,
a ruminant pondering eternity.

Hell and damnation! The novels I've read—
the endless amenities from cover to cover!
And the verses
invoking the May Day!
(I postdate my own May the Second.)

Put it this way: we have
muddied our landscapes,
and the highways that led to the sky
bear down on us all
with the wastes of a spoiling commodity.

The beautiful passes,
bereft, as if all the bidders were gone
and only a bundle, stylishly packaged to order, were left us.

Yet beauty shall stay for the dance
and dance with the least of her wooers
from midnight to dawn.
Nor will any compel her to drink down the real like a doctor's
    prescription
or swallow it whole, like a pill.

The real? It is there,
never doubt it—the power of the real to augment
and enlarge us, to make our teeth chatter,
still able to write on the card of our hunger
an order of bread and an order of soul for the table.

Whisper it out! Say
to the virginal forest:

a que diga en secreto su secreto
y a la verdad: No te detengas tanto
que te endurezcas hasta la mentira.

No soy rector de nada, no dirijo,
y por eso atesoro
las equivocaciones de mi canto.

speak your secret in secret;
and to truth: never withhold what you know
lest you harden the truth in a lie.

I am no one's establishment, I administer
nothing: it suffices to cherish
the equivocal cut of my song.

POR FIN NO HAY NADIE

Por fin no hay nadie, no, no hay voz ni boca,
no hay ojos, manos, pies: todos se fueron,
el día limpio corre con un aro,
el aire frío es un metal desnudo.
Sí, metal, aire y agua, y amarilla
inflorescencia, espesa en su racimo,
algo más, lo tenaz de su perfume,
el patrimonio puro de la tierra.

Dónde está la verdad? Pero la llave
se extravió en un ejército de puertas
y allí está entre las otras,
sin hallar
            nunca más
                        su cerradura.

Por fin,
por eso no hay dónde perder
la llave, la verdad ni la mentira.

Aquí
no hay calle, nadie tiene puertas,
sólo con un temblor se abre la arena.
Y se abre todo el mar, todo el silencio,
el espacio con flores amarillas,
se abre el perfume ciego de la tierra
y como no hay caminos
no vendrá nadie, sólo
la soledad que suena
con canto de campana.

IN THE END THERE IS NOBODY

In the end, there is nobody, no, not a voice or a mouth,
no eyes, fingers, feet: everything passes:
an immaculate day bowls away like a hoop,
the chill in the air strips down to cold metal.
Yes, air, metal, water, and the gold
inflorescence lying packed on the branches,
and something more unplaceable, the perfume's tenacity,
the pure patrimony of earth.

Where did the truth go? The key
was mislaid in an army of doors,
it was there on its ring with the others,
but the lock
      is nowhere
           in the world.

No world
for the key to get lost in, no
true or false, in the end.

The street
never was, no one need boast of the doors,
there is only the sand swinging wide, at a tremor.
The whole sea opens up, all the silence,
the space in the yellow of petals,
the blind perfumes of earth open up;
but never a road,
and nothing returns but
the silence that sings
in the bell-metal.

La Barcarola / Barcarole
1967

Translated by Ben Belitt

COMIENZA LA BARCAROLA

1. *Los Amantes de Capri*

La isla sostiene en su centro el alma como una moneda
que el tiempo y el viento limpiaron dejándola pura
como almendra intacta y agreste cortada en la piel del zafiro
y allí nuestro amor fué la torre invisible que tiembla en el humo,
el orbe vacío detuvo su cola estrellada y la red con los peces del
      cielo
porque los amantes de Capri cerraron los ojos y un ronco
      relámpago clavó en el silbante circuito marino
al miedo que huyó desangrándose y herido de muerte
como la amenaza de un pez espantoso por súbito arpón derrotado:
y luego en la miel oceánica navega la estatua de proa,
desnuda, enlazada por el incitante ciclón masculino.

2. *Descripción de Capri*

La viña en la roca, las grietas del musgo, los muros que enredan
las enredaderas, los plintos de flor y de piedra:
la isla es la cítara que fue colocada en la altura sonora
y cuerda por cuerda la luz ensayó desde el día remoto
su voz, el color de las letras del día,
y de su fragante recinto volaba la aurora
derribando el rocío y abriendo los ojos de Europa.

3. *Los Barcos*

Como en el mercado se tiran al saco carbón y cebollas,
alcohol, parafina, papas, zanahorias, chuletas, aceite, naranjas,
el barco es el vago desorden en donde cayeron
melifluas robustas, hambrientos tahures, popés, mercaderes:
a veces deciden mirar el océano que se ha detenido
como un queso azul que amenaza con ojos espesos

THE BARCAROLE BEGINS

1. *The Lovers of Capri*

The island hoards at its center the spirit of lovers, like a coin
scoured by wind and time's passing, to its integral burnish,
intact and uncouth as an almond, cut into the sapphire's patina;
there the invisible tower of our love trembled up through the
     smoke,
a blank comet steaded its tail in the zodiac, like a netful of fish
in the sky: because the eyes of the lovers of Capri were closed, a
     hoarse bolt of light had pinned down the ocean's whistling
     periphery,
all fear fled away, tracking blood in the wake
of the menace, a sudden harpoon in the side of the seabeast of
     chaos, a deathblow;
and at last, in ambrosial salt, the figurehead rose from the wave, a
swimmer of nakedness, rapt in its masculine cyclone, and
     wreathed.

2. *Description of Capri*

The vine in the rock, fissures cut into musk, the walls laced with
     the web of the
climber, the plinths in the stone and the flowers: the whole
island waits like the frets of a zither in the sonorous altitudes,
light moving wire over wire, improvising through daylight and
     distance
the sound of its voice, the alphabet colors of daylight
from whose fragrant enclaves dawn lifts itself skyward
and flies, dropping dew on a world and opening the eyes of all
     Europe.

3. *The Ships*

Like a shopping bag bulging with onions and coal,
alcohol, paraffin, carrots, potatoes, oranges, meat chops and oil:
the ship is an aimless disorder, a shakedown for whatever
tumbles into its hold: hale and mellifluous ladies, impecunious
     cardsharps, poop decks and storekeepers;

Pablo Neruda / 263

y el terror de lo inmóvil penetra en la frente de los pasajeros:
cada hombre desea gastar los zapatos, los pies y los huesos,
moverse en su horrible infinito hasta que ya no exista.
Termina el peligro, la nave circula en el agua del círculo,
y lejos asoman las torres de plata de Montevideo.

4. El Canto

La torre del pan, la estructura que el arco construye en la altura
con la melodía elevando su fértil firmeza
y el pétalo duro del canto creciendo en la rosa,
así tu presencia y tu ausencia y el peso de tu cabellera,
el fresco calor de tu cuerpo de avena en la cama,
la piel victoriosa que tu primavera dispuso al costado
de mi corazón que golpeaba en la piedra del muro,
el firme contacto de trigo y de oro de tus asoledas caderas,
tu voz derramando dulzura salvaje como una cascada,
tu boca que amó la presión de mis besos tardíos,
fué como si el día y la noche cortaran su nudo mostrando
    entreabierta,
la puerta que une y separa a la luz de la sombra
y por la abertura asomara el distante dominio
que el hombre buscaba picando la piedra, la sombra, el vacío.

5. La Chascona

La piedra y los clavos, la tabla, la teja se unieron: he aquí
    levantada
la casa chascona con agua que corre escribiendo en su idioma,
las zarzas guardaban el sitio con su sanguinario ramaje
hasta que la escala y sus muros supieron tu nombre
y la flor encrespada, la vid y su alado zarcillo,
las hojas de higuera que como estandartes de razas remotas
cernían sus alas oscuras sobre tu cabeza,

sometimes they stop to squint back at the custodial water
looking cheesy and blue and opaque with a menace of eyes:
a fear of the motionless, bores through to the voyager's fantasy.
They would rather wear out their shoe leather, whittle down their
    feet and their bones,
keep on the move, in infinity's horror, till nothing is left of it.
But the danger subsides: the ship circles its watery circle
and beyond it, the silvery towers of Montevideo heave to.

4. *The Song*

The tower of bread, the device that the archway contrives out of
    altitude
with a melody moving aloft in its avid fecundity,
the intransigent petals of song growing big in the rose
—your presence and absence, the whole weight of your hair,
the pure heats of your body like a pillar of grain in my bed,
the victorious skin that your springtime aligned at my side
while my heart beat below like a pulse in the stone of a wall,
wheaten and gold in the power of its contacts, your sunburst of
    hips,
and your voice flowing down in cascades of a vehement honey,
your mouth turned in love for the gradual pressure of kisses
—all seems to me now like the knot of the day and the night, cut
    through, and showing
the door that unites and divides light and shade, ajar on its hinges,
and beyond it, in the spaces, a glimpse of that distant dominion
man seeks his whole lifetime, hacking away at the stone and the
    dark and the void.

5. *"La Chascona"**

Boulder and nail, the plank and the tile are here joined: I have
    built
out of water that writes all things down in its cursive calligraphy
    La Casa Chascona;

---

* Literally, "Girl with the Wild Hair"; see note, "To 'La Sebastiana,'" p. 157.
"Chascona," a word unique to Chile, applies to all that is unkempt and
disheveled.

el muro de azul victorioso, el ónix abstracto del suelo,
tus ojos, mis ojos, están derramados en roca y madera
por todos los sitios, los días febriles, la paz que construye,
y sigue ordenada la casa con tu transparencia.
Mi casa, tu casa, tu sueño en mis ojos, tu sangre siguiendo el
          camino del cuerpo que duerme
como una paloma cerrada en sus alas inmóvil persigue su vuelo
y el tiempo recoge en su copa tu sueño y el mío
en la casa que apenas nació de las manos despiertas.

La noche encontrada por fin en la nave que tú construimos,
la paz de madera olorosa que sigue con pájaros
que sigue el susurro del viento perdido en las hojas
y de las raíces que comen la paz suculenta del humus
mientras sobreviene sobre mí dormida la luna del agua
como una paloma del bosque del Sur que dirige el dominio
del cielo, del aire, del viento sombrío que te pertenece,
dormida durmiendo en la casa que hicieron tus manos,
delgada en el sueño, en el germen del humus nocturno
y multiplicada en la sombra como el crecimiento del trigo.

Dorada, la tierra te dió la armadura del trigo,
el color que los hornos cocieron con barro y delicia,
la piel que no es blanca ni es negra ni roja ni verde
que tiene el color de la arena, del pan, de la lluvia,
del sol, de la pura madera, del viento,
tu carne color de campana, color de alimento fragante,
tu carne que forma la nave y encierra la ola!

De tantas delgadas estrellas que mi alma recoge en la noche
recibo el rocío que el día convierte en ceniza
y bebo la copa de estrellas difuntas llorando las lágrimas
de todos los hombres, de los prisioneros, de los carceleros,
y todas las manos me buscan mostrando una llaga,
mostrando el dolor, el suplicio o la brusca esperanza
y así sin que el cielo y la tierra me dejen tranquilo,
así consumido por otros dolores que cambian de rostro.
Recibo en el sol y en el día la estatua de tu claridad

I have planted the berry and blood of the thicket to keep watch
on this place till its stairways and walls know you by name, till
the flower crisping its petals, the vine, and the feathering tendrils,
the fig leaf like a heraldry raised on the alien life of a clan
blossom like wings in the shadow that darkens your head:
the walls of victorious blue, the abstract onyx of earth—
your eyes and mine—here break on this rock and this timber
in the name of all places and time's fever and the peace we have
    won,
to preside on a house's successions in your person's transparency.
Your house and mine, your dream in my eyes, your blood on the
    paths of the body asleep
like a pigeon locked into its wings' immobility and its flying
    momentum;
time gathers your dream and mine in its cup
for a house barely born to the world from the vigil of hands.

Night brings us at last to the ship we have fashioned together,
the repose of the sweet-smelling wood where a backwash
of wind and birds lost to us, lives again in the leaves,
the roots crop the succulent peace of the humus,
and the moon climbs the water to accomplish my slumber,
the meridional dove of the forests whose dominion
is heaven and air and the somnolent wind which commends
you, a dreamer asleep in the house and the work of your hands,
now so slight in your dream, in the seed of the humus's midnight,
yet multiplied there in the dark like a harvest of wheat.

Beloved and golden, earth gave you wheat's armor,
a color that ovens bake in the clay, with the sweets and enamels,
that singular skin neither black, white, red, green,
but hued like the sand, the bread crust, the rain,
the sun and the wind and the cut in the virginal timber,
a flesh, bell-colored, colored like savory grains,
yet shaped by a ship's keel and enclosed in a wave.

All that delicate light my soul gathered up from the stars,
the gifts of the dew and the night, are transformed into ashes
    by day:

Pablo Neruda / 267

y en la sombra, en la luna, en el sueño, el racimo del reino,
el contacto que induce a mi sangre a cantar en la muerte.

La miel, bienamada, la ilustre dulzura del viaje completo
y aún, entre largos caminos, fundamos en Valparaíso una torre,
por más que en tus pies encontré mis raíces perdidas
tú y yo mantuvimos abierta la puerta del mar insepulto
y así destinamos a la Sebastiana el deber de llamar los navíos
y ver bajo el humo del puerto la rosa incitante,
el camino cortado en el agua por el hombre y sus mercaderías.

Pero azul y rosado, roído y amargo entreabierto entre sus telarañas
he aquí, sosteniéndose en hilos, en uñas, en enredaderas,
he aquí, victorioso, harapiento, color de campana y de miel,
he aquí, bermellón y amarillo, purpúreo, plateado, violeta,
sombrío y alegre, secreto y abierto como una sandía
el puerto y la puerta de Chile, el manto radiante de Valparaíso,
el sonoro estupor de la lluvia en los cerros cargados de
    padecimientos
el sol resbalando en la oscura mirada, en los ojos más bellos del
    mundo.

Yo te convidé a la alegría de un puerto agarrado a la furia del alto
    oleaje
metido en el frío del último océano, viviendo en peligro,
hermosa es la nave sombría, la luz vesperal de los meses antárticos,
la nave de techo amaranto, el puñado de velas o casas o vidas
que aquí se vistieron con trajes de honor y banderas
y se sostuvieron cayéndose en el terremoto que abría y cerraba el
    infierno,
tomándose al fin de la mano los hombres, los muros, las cosas,
unidos y desvencijados en el estertor planetario.

I drink from a dead planet's cup amidst weeping and tears,
the tears of all men and their griefs: the prisoner's tears and the
    jailer's,
all hands lifted up to me, showing the sore's
suppuration, woe or entreaty or importunate hope:
no respite from heaven or earth—
one terror feeds on another and is changed in its turn.
There is only your clarity under the sun, day's figurehead,
the flowering branch of your kingdom in darkness, in the moon,
    in a dream
at whose touch my blood comes alive and sings in the kingdoms
    of death.

The packed honeycomb, the radiant sweets of the consummate
    voyage,
my darling: here, after long roadways we have planted a tower
    in Valparaíso:
here at your feet I have found my lost
roots: together we open the seaport, unconfined, together
we charge the Sebastiana* to summon the navies
and display in the smoke of the port the rose's excitement,
the lanes carved in water for the movement of men and
    commodities.

Pink and blue, worm-eaten and sour, swinging ajar on its
    filaments,
looped on its threads and its thorns and its matted entanglements,
triumphant and beggarly here, colored like bells or like honey,
vermilion and yellow and purple, violet and silver,
joyless or joyful, sealed or slashed open, like a melon,
here is the port and the doorway to Chile, the bright cloak of
    Valparaíso,
the sonorous stupor of rain on a saddle of hills like a sufferer's
burden, sun vying with shade in the loveliest eyes in the world.

For you, all the furors and joys of a seaport that grapples
the breakers' successions, drenched in the freeze of mid-ocean,
    acquainted

---

* See note: "To 'La Sebastiana,'" p. 157.

with peril: comely, that vessel's sobriety; comely the months of
　　the vesperal light of
Antarctica, the ship roofed with amaranth, the hand's strength in
　　our sails and our houses
and lives, each arrayed in the cloths of its status, pennants
　　displayed,
intact in the pull of the vortices, earthquakes that open and shut
　　their infernos,
hand clasping hand in the harbors; walls, people, and artifacts
joined in one body, atremble on a rattletrap planet.

SELECTED BIBLIOGRAPHY

1921   *La canción de la fiesta (Fiesta Song)*. Santiago de Chile, Federación de Estudiantes de Chile.

1923   *Crespusculario (Twilight Book)*. Santiago de Chile, Revista *Claridad* de la Federación de Estudiantes de Chile.

1924   *Veinte poemas de amor y una canción desesperada (Twenty Love Poems and A Desperate Song)*. Santiago de Chile, Nascimento.

1925   *Tentativa del hombre infinito (Venture of Infinite Man)*. Santiago de Chile, Nascimento.

         El habitante y su esperanza (Sojourner and his Hope). Prose. Santiago de Chile, Nascimento.

1926   *Anillos (Rings)*. Prose. Santiago de Chile, Nascimento.

1933   *El hondero entusiasta (The Slinger-Enthusiast)*. Santiago de Chile, Empresa Letras.

         Residencia en la tierra (Residence on Earth). Santiago de Chile, Nascimento.

1935   *Residencia en la tierra. I y II (1925-1935) (Residence on Earth)*. In two volumes. Madrid, Cruz y Raya.

         Visiones de las hijas de Albión y El viajero mental, de William Blake (Visions of the Daughters of Albion and *The Mental Traveler,* by William Blake). Translation. Madrid, Cruz y Raya.

1937   *España en el corazón (Spain in the Heart)*. Santiago de Chile, Ercilla.

1939   *Las furias y las penas (The Woes and the Furies)*. Santiago de Chile, Nascimento.

1947   *Tercera residencia, 1935-1945 (Residence on Earth, III)*. Buenos Aires, Losada.

1950	*Canto general (General Song)*. Mexico, D.F., Talleres Gráficos de la Nación.
1951	*Poesías completas (Complete Poems)*. Buenos Aires, Losada.
1954	*Las uvas y el viento (The Grapes and the Wind)*. Santiago de Chile, Nascimento.
	Odas elementales (Elemental Odes). Buenos Aires, Losada.
1956	*Nuevas odas elementales (New Elemental Odes)*. Buenos Aires, Losada.
1957	*Obras completas (Complete Works)*. Buenos Aires, Losada.
	Tercer libro de las odas (Third Book of Odes). Buenos Aires, Losada.
1958	*Estravagario (Book of Vagaries)*. Buenos Aires, Losada.
1959	*Navegaciones y regresos (Voyages and Homecomings)*. Buenos Aires, Losada.
1960	*Cien sonetos de amor (One Hundred Love Sonnets)*. Buenos Aires, Losada.
	Las piedras de Chile (The Stones of Chile). Buenos Aires, Losada.
1961	*Cantos ceremoniales (Ceremonial Songs)*. Buenos Aires, Losada.
1962	*Plenos poderes (Full Powers)*. Buenos Aires, Losada.
1964	*Memorial de Isla Negra (Black Island Memorial)*. Buenos Aires, Losada.
1967	*La barcarola (Barcarole)*. Buenos Aires, Losada.
1968	*Las manos del día (The Hands of Day)*. Buenos Aires, Losada.

DATE DUE